SECRETS

of a
Strong Mind

What My Years As An FBI
Counterintelligence Agent Taught Me
About Leadership and Empowerment—
And How To Make It Work For YOU

LaRae Quy

ISBN-10: 1479134708
EAN-13: 978-1479134700

TABLE OF CONTENTS

SECRETS

of a

Strong Mind

What My Years As An FBI Counterintelligence Agent
Taught Me About Leadership and Empowerment—
And How To Make It Work For You

INTRODUCTION

I spent over twenty years working as an FBI undercover and counterintelligence agent. I completed new agent's training in 1983 and retired in 2006. My job was to identify foreign spies who were operating in the United States, find out what they were stealing and stop them, assess whether they possessed the type of information the U.S. needed, and if they did, find ways to persuade them to work for our government.

Faced with stressful and fast-moving situations, I needed to move through many different barriers to succeed. Barriers come in all shapes and forms. For some, it is a self-limiting belief; for others, it is a glass ceiling. A Strong Mind is the birthplace of personal leadership development. It is the ability for each person to look inward and find solid ground when the going gets tough because most barriers are internal, not external.

In this book, I'll talk about specific cases I worked on, how I worked them, and whether or not they were successful. All names have been changed to protect the identities of individuals involved in my cases. I will share the lessons I learned about surviving in an environment of deception, hostility, and fear. Coincidentally, these same conditions also exist in business and life, and they can create barriers to our success.

If you are going to survive in today's world, you will need to learn how to navigate through the confusion that exists in relationships, investments, and business. Often, we have very little control over our environment. Even the best of plans can fail because people, markets, and business are not predictable.

Strong minds are flexible enough to act in the moment. As I learned as an FBI agent, it was essential for my survival to have a mind that was strong and flexible so I could respond from a place of strength.

Adversity can come in the shape of personal and career setbacks, grief and loss, new challenges, or periods of transition. Research[1] has shown that most people, when confronted with adversity and the need to survive in fast-moving and challenging environments, will experience initial feelings of fear, frustration, and paralysis. Given sufficient amounts of time, however, they recover and continue to perform at the same level they were performing before the adversity.

At one end of the continuum there are a small percentage of people who do not bounce back and remain unable to cope with their circumstances without assistance. They often need counseling and can experience breakdowns.

On the other end of the continuum, however, are those with strong minds who not only survive adverse and traumatic situations, but also thrive and grow. In this book I will discuss the components that comprise a strong mind. In each chapter readers will be given a set of tactics to help them uncover their own personal strengths.

A strong mind can be taught and learned. I learned how to develop a strong mind in my career as an FBI undercover and counterintelligence agent. Most of the secrets in this book about how to do so are primarily those I learned from my FBI experiences. I also share how my childhood and background influenced the way I interpreted the lessons I learned as an FBI agent.

A strong mind will empower the leader in you. Leadership is a journey that begins with self—whether we are leading corporations, a small business, or a household. Some have called it a hero's journey because it requires the strength to explore our beliefs and let them go if they've outlived their usefulness. A journey requires us to go deep and become intimate with the hidden parts of ourselves; to expand the boundaries of who we believe we are and move beyond the limitations we've placed around ourselves.

Empowerment is a journey to the interior. It discovers what is really lurking beneath the surface, the part of us that we don't often let others see—even ourselves! This book will show you ways to say yes to the adventure of the journey. This is the true definition of leadership: it is not what you know; it is *how* you are when facing the unknown.

A key to developing a strong mind is identifying patterns of behavior, something critical in all successful FBI investigations. Successful agents quickly become experts at identifying patterns, not only those of the subjects under investigation, but of their own as well. These behaviors either help or hinder us in getting what we want. Once you identify your unproductive patterns of behavior, you have the tool that empowers you to make changes in your life—you can make better choices in the way you respond to situations.

We are all creatures of habit; we tend to repeat what works. More often than not, we also tend to repeat what does not work simply because we stop observing our behavior with a critical eye. We get lazy and become complacent, but as I have learned, in volatile and rapidly changing environments, complacency will lead to extinction.

When confronted with rapid shifts, ambiguity and deceptive environments, we need to land on solid ground. Strong minds understand that the solid ground is inside of us. Once we understand how to access that solid ground when the going gets tough, we can move forward from a place of confidence.

The core secrets to a strong mind are authenticity, purpose, courage, confidence, determination, and resilience. In this book we will spend a chapter exploring each one and finding ways to develop them in a way that is unique and personal to you.

The goal of this book is to show how to develop a strong mind by embracing and learning from challenges to become an empowered leader. And a strong mind is essential to becoming a strong leader.

FEATURES TO HELP YOU

In the TACTICS section that follows each chapter, I am going to ask that you do your own sleuthing and make yourself the subject of your own investigation. The TACTICS will help you probe beneath the surface to peel back the layers of truth about yourself. Collect data to find out what is true and what works for you. It is not enough to identify what you want to change. If it were, New Year's resolutions would be a panacea. I believe the best way to improve your chances at success is to see how and why you are not successful in areas that are important to you. Self-knowledge is the foundation of leadership and empowerment.

The TACTICS are optional. If they do not speak to you now, give them a pass. You can always address them later when you have more time. Each set of TACTICS will help you uncover the truth as it applies to you so you can develop a strong mind.

You will also find:

Point to Ponder: Each section will be summarized in a single sentence for you to ponder over during your day or week.
Inspiration: This will be a quote to inspire you that summarizes a truth from the section you've just read.
Reflection Question: These questions will help you think further about ways you can develop a strong mind. Write down the answers in a journal or somewhere you can easily access them. Writing down answers helps to clarify your thoughts.

CHAPTER 1
AUTHENTICITY

"What lies behind us and what lies ahead of us are tiny matters compared to what lies within us."

— RALPH WALDO EMERSON

While assigned to my first FBI office in Phoenix, Arizona, a fellow agent working undercover on a criminal case asked me to pose as his girlfriend for an afternoon BBQ at the home of one of his targets—a man suspected of involvement with organized crime. The undercover operation had been going on for several months so the undercover agent (referred to as the UCA) had been able to meet several prominent members of the gang. I met with the undercover agent and his supervisor before the BBQ to discuss the goals of the afternoon.

The plan was simple: I was to accompany the UCA as a casual friend and attempt to gather background information on as many individuals attending the BBQ as possible. The UCA, meanwhile, would spend his time trying to inveigle his way into the group's confidence so he would be invited to future get-togethers. The FBI viewed this group as unpredictable because we knew they would be suspicious of federal agents trying to infiltrate their inner circle. They were also on the lookout for rival gangs trying to infiltrate their criminal organization. For this reason, the plan was for us to stay together and help support each other's stories. Being new to the group, I was assured that I'd be safe in case something unexpected did happen.

It sounded like a solid plan—to me, but then I was twenty-five years old and only a few months out of the FBI Academy, so I didn't even know what questions to ask the supervisor. Plans are essential, but when you're dealing with volatile environments, the situation can change in an instant. This one did.

We left our guns at home and took fake driver's licenses with us instead. I was not certain how to dress for a BBQ with an organized crime gang, so I decided to wear what I would normally wear for an outdoor event—crop pants, sandals, and a white t-shirt.

We arrived at a single-level ranch house built on a corner lot. As we entered, several women greeted us with a cigarette in one hand and a beer in the other. A small blonde woman stepped up, placed her cigarette in her mouth, and took my handbag with her free hand. Without smiling or saying a word, I watched as she headed off to one of the bedrooms. I made a mental note to check on whether the piece of thin black thread I had woven into the zipper would still be in place when I got it back. No one could unzip the handbag without disturbing the thread.

A tall, thin man with balding hair smiled and welcomed us. Dressed in jeans and a leather vest open to the waist with nothing on underneath but tattoos in the shape of serpents, he handed me a can of beer. The UCA and I joined a group of approximately twenty-five people in the backyard. A six-foot fence made the yard extremely private from street traffic.

After an hour or so of introductions and casual banter, I went to find my handbag for sunscreen. I found two women in a bedroom/TV room huddled around some items on a desk, my handbag among them. I smiled, joined them, and reached for my sunscreen.

> Three men followed me into the room and closed the door behind them. I was thus isolated in a room with three men and two women who associated with drug dealers, extortionists, and occasionally, murderers.

Becoming separated and isolated from my UCA "date" was definitely not part of the plan. I had no way to communicate to him and didn't know how things were going at his end.

We in the room somehow began talking about cross-country motorcycle racing, but I was clearly their focus. They were suspicious, I knew—this was an opportunity for the target and his minions to look my fellow agent over (and me) to determine whether we could be vetted and trusted or identified as federal agents. As I stood in that room, alone, I knew I could never pretend to develop rapport with them, so I stayed as close as possible to my real personality and background.

The conversation moved to me, and they asked me where I came from. I told them about my upbringing on a cattle ranch in Wyoming. I said I spent summers greasing bailers and digging fence pole holes. The guy with the leather vest said, "Awesome." I picked up on that word and repeated it, only this time as a question. The conversation at once turned to him and now he was the one explaining what he thought was awesome.

One of the men asked me why I left home and came to Arizona to go to college. I said, "I didn't want my life to fall into a rut. There's a time to get out, and if I didn't make that move, I might never get away." This response came from a place of transparency and honesty on my part.

The small blonde woman who had taken my handbag at the door blurted out, "But here we are." I knew her answer also came from a place of honesty, although her subsequent remarks sounded supportive of her situation and friends. In that second, however, I knew she felt trapped in her situation. The two of us had a common bond.

I paid close attention to their body language. While the men were the ones to dominate the conversation, it was the small blonde woman who was calling the shots. She signaled that it was time to move on by walking over and opening the door. I made sure I wasn't the first one to follow her out, but sighed with relief when I was out. I felt I had passed a crucial test. My fellow agent, however, failed to grasp that the group was already suspicious of him. He stuck to the plan and talked, postured, and tried to persuade the target they were both good old boys with similar interests.

After the UCA and I left, I checked to see whether the thin black thread was still woven into the zipper of my handbag. It was not. When my handbag had been searched, it had fallen into the bottom of my bag. Otherwise, nothing was out of place or looked disturbed.

A few weeks later I learned from the UCA's supervisor that the criminal gang suspected the UCA of being a member of a rival gang. An FBI informant, who was a trusted member of the gang hosting the BBQ, reported that plans were made within days of the afternoon event to kill the UCA. He was briskly pulled out of the undercover operation and transferred to another city. The informant made no mention of me, however, and I believe they never suspected me because, in spite of using another name, I wasn't trying to be anyone other than who I really am. My conversations with these people were very real and honest.

I was being authentic.

The informant was able to provide the FBI with enough probable cause to issue a search warrant on the house where the BBQ was held. Arrest warrants followed, and the tall, thin man with the leather vest and serpent tattoos was charged with extortion, drug dealing, and obstruction of justice.

AUTHENTICITY MATTERS

Trying to be someone else is a waste of time.

Authenticity is the ability to share the deepest and truest part of ourselves with others regardless of the situation. Authenticity begins with knowing who we are and what we believe.

The moral of that one FBI experience is this: never try to be someone other than who you are. You may not find yourself surrounded by violent members of organized crime, but competitors who want to "take out" your business may be all around you. You may never need to talk yourself out of a desperate situation with criminals, but getting people to trust you is important in business and personal life.

My undergraduate degree at Northern Arizona University was in Business Management. The first thing we did in class was to identify successful leaders and write papers on how to mimic their behaviors. Textbooks were full of tips on how to do this and tests made certain we ingested the critical points. They helped, but only to a point.

> My success as an undercover agent came
> from being myself—it attracted people to me.
> The only time I really ran into trouble was
> when I didn't take the time to be authentic.
> The game was up.

It happened several years ago when I worked an undercover operation jointly with the CIA against a foreign spy. My role was to be an expert in marketing while my male CIA counterpart's role was to be a successful investor in emerging technologies. I studied and talked to several people about the traits of good advertising programs and prepared as much as I could within the short time frame. I showed up at the meeting wearing a nice suit with no changes to my regular hair and make-up routine. My male CIA counterpart, however, wore a false moustache, dyed hair, and a Southern accent.

As we entered conversations with the spy, my comments about successful advertising plans lacked innovation and passion. I sounded as though I was selling a product that even I wouldn't buy. My CIA partner didn't sound much better. The jargon he used came from too many issues of Harvard Business Review. As a result, the entire evening was a waste of time because the spy never re-initiated contact.

In subsequent undercover operations, I made sure that my cover story was rooted in authentic experience and emotions. It was ridiculous for me to pretend to be an engineer or advertising executive. Instead, I wove my personal experiences into my cover story and stayed as close to the real LaRae as possible in all of my interactions. I got much better results because I was responding from a place that was real and not fake. I never ventured far from my business background in retail or my graduate studies at Arizona State University in persuasion and communication. I always stayed true to my upbringing on a cattle ranch in Wyoming.

> Being honest with others is not dependent upon the situation because an authentic person knows who they are in any given moment. They don't flit from one belief system to another because of a fad, pressure from others, or circumstances.

After I retired from the FBI, I completed a three-year graduate program in Spiritual Direction at San Francisco Theological

Seminary. I found that seminary classes teaching how to get beneath people's layers of denial and uncover the truth about themselves involved using many of the same skills I had developed as an FBI agent.

BE AUTHENTIC

To be authentic, I needed to be the best version of me. Here is how I did it:

Discover strengths and manage weaknesses. In my early years, I was eager to take personality tests like Myers Briggs so I could peek inside my psyche and pinpoint my strongest personality traits. If I were not sure about one of them, I would talk to friends who knew me well and who were willing to help me explore them. The emphasis was on reinforcing my strengths with practice and learning.

Later, strategists like Marcus Buckingham came along with books like, *Now, Discover Your Strengths*, and suggested that we manage our weaknesses instead of trying to turn them into strengths. I have always believed that my greatest room for growth is in the areas of my greatest strengths, and I minimize the time I waste in developing a weakness. In other words, I don't worry about what was left out; I work on what was left in.

It's stupid to ignore a weakness, however. I had to acknowledge that I could not be talented in all areas. I needed to find ways to free up my time so I could hone my strengths. Ironically, if I ignored one of my strengths, it became a weakness if not managed properly.

> You are as strong as your greatest strength. You are always stronger than your weaknesses.

Identify the vulnerability. At quite a young age, I saw a mountain lion run down a deer fawn and kill it. I still hear the screams the baby animal made as it died. I believed I had witnessed vulnerability—and I wanted nothing to do with it. There was not only danger, but also shame in being defenseless and exposed. In my imagination, I saw a buck deer spring to the defense of the fawn and fight off the mountain lion with its horns. In my naiveté, I associated a protected environment with being in control—the opposite of vulnerability.

I tried to maintain control by erecting barriers around me while in college and early in my career. But I learned that isolation from others does not guarantee a stable and protected environment. Instead, it became a downward spiral as the isolation made me feel even more vulnerable! It wasn't until I joined a discipleship group in my local church that I understood the importance of connecting with others in a deep and meaningful way.

By sharing with others, I learned that vulnerability was not about finding a way to protect myself; it was about becoming more self-aware. And knowledge is power. By being vulnerable, I learned ways to break old habits, conquer fear, find my focus, and manage stress. I understood why I gave in to temptation and how I could find the strength to resist. Later, in situations like the one I described earlier in the chapter, I realized that I was strong enough to be vulnerable. I knew myself well enough that I was in charge of my choices.

Develop a strong connection between values and behavior. I committed myself to my personal values. I found ways to go over, around, or through them. My path did not always look like I thought it would at the end, but this is where mental toughness gave me the ability to adapt to changing circumstances. I never forget that my behavior reflects my values.

Build relationships with a diverse group of friends and associates. Create genuine relationships by being authentic. Authenticity builds trust and makes us more compelling and attractive leaders. Be prepared for the adversaries who will be created because you've remained true to your values and beliefs. Remember that leadership is not about being popular.

Mental toughness starts with being authentic, and the key components of authenticity are personal values, inner vision, and self-awareness.

THINKING ABOUT AUTHENTIC SELF

Point to Ponder: In a world where you can be anything, be yourself.

Inspiration: *"Hard times arouse an instinctive desire for authenticity."*—Coco Chanel

Reflection Question: How can I be the best version of me?

PERSONAL VALUES

*"Education without values, as useful as it is,
seems rather to make man a more clever devil."*

— C.S. LEWIS

We make choices based on what is important to us.

As a new FBI agent reporting into my first office in Phoenix, I was assigned to the Bank Robbery squad. Very often the description of a bank robber was sketchy at best because most of them tried to hide or disguise their face in some way. We called them "UNSUBS" or unidentified subjects and they made up a large number of our caseload.

The squad had posted sketches in local newspapers, television stations, and post offices of an UNSUB suspect in a recent bank robbery from a nearby state in the hopes he might be recognized. A few days later, the office received a tip from a citizen that an individual matching the UNSUB's description was spotted at a nightclub in the downtown area. Five members of our squad rendezvoused nearby and waited until the FBI surveillance team had identified the individual who resembled the UNSUB.

A couple of my fellow agents and myself approached the guy. He was clean-shaven and dressed in jeans, red sweater, and white running shoes that looked new. I stood back ready to draw my gun while the other two agents patted the man down for a concealed weapon. They found nothing. They asked him for his identification and he pulled out a driver's license from a neighboring state.

A computer check of his identification came back without any outstanding arrest warrants, and while there was a resemblance to the UNSUB wanted for the bank robbery, none of us could tell whether it was him, so the consensus was to let him go.

One agent, however, was more diligent. Fingerprints of the UNSUB had been lifted from the bank's countertop and forwarded to our squad. The agent suggested manually matching up fingerprints. It's a labor intensive and tedious way to match fingerprints in this day and age, but we did not have enough probable cause to arrest him and thus get the electronically read fingerprints.

All five FBI agents were now surrounding the man, so when the agent asked if we could look at his fingers, he did not object. We moved outside where the lighting was better. My training agent, Ron, told two of the younger agents and me to stand back and be alert in case the man tried to bolt. Ron held the fingerprints we had on file under the light with one hand; in the other, he held the flashlight and shined it on the man's hand. The other agent took the man's fingers, one at a time, in his hands and stretched out the finger pads to make it easier to read the fingerprints manually. He visually matched the whorls on the UNSUB's finger with the fingerprints we had on file. Lo and behold, it was a match!

My attitude shifted a little that day, and the importance of perseverance and determination climbed a little higher on my list of personal values.

THE POWER OF PERSONAL VALUES

Who was I becoming?

It was not a question I'd given much thought to until this incident. In fact, I had not even thought about the role personal values played in my choices in life, much less identify the most important ones to me. My parents had instilled in me at a young age a strong moral sense of right and wrong, but since others had prescribed these values, I had no ownership of them for myself.

"You have brains in your head and feet in your shoes
You can steer yourself in any direction you choose.
You're on your own and you know what you know
And you are the one who'll decide where you'll go."

— DR. SEUSS

With the accretion of time and experience, I chose my personal values and then linked my behavior to them. Values have guided my life with intention and purpose.

They will help you do the following:

Create a clear guideline for actions. Ironically, I found authenticity to be the most important component while working as an undercover FBI agent. It's easy to slap on a different name and job title. From organized drug gangs to Russian spies, I found the most convincing way to develop relationships with them was to be honest about who I was as a person by sharing my values and the truest part of myself.

14

You will be less likely to chase after something that does not fit into what you truly want to accomplish in life. Once you know what you do want, you know how to move toward it with intention.

Help you make good choices. When isolated in a room as an undercover agent with the three men and two women associated with organized crime, it was not difficult for me to make a decision on how to move forward: I would be honest and not try to be someone I was not.

One of the men asked me what brought me to his city and I told him that I transferred to the state university. While he couldn't relate to my desire to get away from my old sorority life, he could relate to how it felt to get away from the rut that I felt as a young adult. I talked about my love of dogs and gardening. I even talked about my faith journey, which was a surprising hit with a couple of them.

I told them I was burning to do something bigger and better with my life than what I knew as a child. One of the women felt the same way—I could tell by the way she fell quiet.

I made the right choices that day by linking my behavior to my values.

Good choices are those that are consistent with your personal values. When you know what's most important to you, making a decision is quite simple.

Most people cannot make decisions because they aren't clear on what is important to them. Clear values provide clarity in your decisions.

Live authentically. Live true to your values and you will feel more at peace. You will also feel more fulfilled because you are being true to yourself.

My top five values are integrity, perseverance, adventure, intelligence, and spirituality. Whichever way I moved forward in my undercover situation, it would be with determination, honesty, and honor.

OWNERSHIP OF VALUES

Live your life on purpose.

The focus on what you are going to do in life begins very early and stays with you for most of your adult life. The question of who you are going to become in that process is often ignored—until a crisis reminds you that life is not always as fulfilling as you had dreamed it would be. Crisis can be a death in the family, divorce, personal conflict, unemployment, or simply coming to the realization "life is what happened when you were busy making other plans."

As leaders, it's important to recognize the values we portray in our leadership. Whether we lead a team of hundreds or an army of one, our reputation as a leader is at risk if we're unable to effectively convey our personal values to others. This requires that we not only acknowledge them, but also find ways for our life to reflect them.

Personal values are unique and deep-rooted in each one of us. Many of us find ourselves too busy to take the time to consider how our values impact the way we live out our lives. In fact, there's a good chance that some of us would be hard pressed to name our personal values if asked to write them down.

I worked as a manager at a department store for a few years after college. Every year we had to endure the annual inventory of stock. In essence, we compared what we actually owned to what we thought we owned. If you were to take inventory of your life over the past year, how did your personal values help you make the best decisions and wise moral choices? A review of our personal inventory not only reminds us of the values we have in stock and at our disposal, but also of how many of them have shifted over time.

THINKING ABOUT PERSONAL VALUES

Point to Ponder: The direction of my life is controlled by my values.

Inspiration: *"It's not hard to make decisions when you know what your values are."*—Roy Disney

Reflection Question: How have your personal values helped you make the best decisions and wise moral choices for yourself?

INNER VISION

"At the center of your being
you have the answer;
you know who you are
and you know what you want."
—LAO TZU

As a counterintelligence agent, I persuaded foreign spies to work for the U. S. government. I learned to be a patient observer of human behavior by putting the targets of my investigation under surveillance and watching their movements for months at a time. My job was to get inside their heads and construct a personality assessment before I ever met them. It can take several years to recruit a spy, and more than once in my career I sat in the FBI's Behavioral Science Unit in Quantico, Virginia to gain clarity on the target's personal values, goals, and beliefs.

It is difficult for most of us to have perfect clarity about our own lives, and we are the ones living it! It becomes therefore extremely difficult to look into someone else's mind and sort out their fears, desires, and motivations.

I will share the story of George (not his real name.) He was a diminutive man in his mid-30's, who wore thick, black plastic framed glasses that hid his gray eyes; he brushed his thinning, brown hair straight back. The assignment to the San Francisco Russian Consulate as a Political Officer would provide the opportunity he had long sought to raise himself out of the gray masses of the Soviet Union's post-Stalin era in the early 1980s.

The only way to get ahead in those days was to join the Communist Party. Since George had big plans for his life, he became a party member while enrolled at a university in St. Petersburg. George was both intelligent and hardworking. He came to the attention of university officials, who reminded him that while the Communist Party was willing to offer a helping hand with his education and career, it also expected a quid pro quo. The choice for George was simple: stay behind and remain an impoverished engineer, or join the elite ranks of the KGB. Although he knew he would always be an engineer first and a spy second, George grabbed the lifeline.

In the 1980s, President Mikhail Gorbachev was making overtures to move the Soviet Union out of the Cold War, but a dash of openness can be a dangerous thing for an autocratic state. The slice of daylight over the gray masses doubled back like a heat-seeking missile, ending the Soviet Union and opening up endless possibilities for a man like George. Once the Soviet Union's largest state had become Russia, the KGB changed its name to the more user-friendly FSB in an effort to shed its former reputation; but the game was still the same. Stealing U.S. military, economic, and political secrets remained a top priority for Russian spies. George was sent to San Francisco, where the Silicon Valley was bursting with classified research, think tanks, and proprietary technology.

The FBI was on the lookout. The FBI received information from a sensitive source that George was a KGB officer. Once he was identified as a Russian spy, a case agent was chosen from the Bureau's counter-intelligence squads in San Francisco. I was that agent.

I interviewed the people with whom he was in contact and analyzing his every move. He was under surveillance wherever he went and I would follow up and interview the people he met. I also had informants attached to the think tanks in the Bay Area who reported on George's activities and contacts.

Tapped telephones and undercover agents came next. Needless to say, the KGB had trained George to expect our attempts either to recruit him to work for the U.S. or to catch him in the act of spying. If caught, he would have been thrown out of the country and disgraced upon his return home. The thought of that, for someone like George, was unbearable.

George had been trained by the best to keep a low profile. He was careful. He didn't make quick friends with Americans because he knew they could either be informants for the FBI, or worse—undercover agents. George and his KGB trainers had watched too many American movies and read too many spy thrillers to know reality. They had developed a stereotype of what the typical FBI agent looks like: gun toting, polyester clad investigator who wore cheap shoes and drove American-made cars. George had been taught that one of the best ways to avoid detection was to network only with Americans who had already been vetted by a seasoned FSB officer. His predecessor in San Francisco, another Russian spy, introduced George to his network of trusted contacts before he left for Moscow.

One of them was a mild-mannered American who wore Italian suits, drove German cars, and got weekly manicures. He was erudite and spoke eloquently about the importance of being true to our passions and following our dreams. Rarely did the conversation veer from the topics of philosophy and personal growth. He seldom voiced a political viewpoint. George came to feel a deep bond of trust with his suave new friend; he not only confided his dreams and aspirations to this man, but bared his soul to him.

Unfortunately for George, this man was also an FBI undercover agent. Together, the agent and I wove a web so tightly around George that he was unable to discern where reality left off and illusion began.

Little by little, I learned that he came from a poor area of Russia. George's parents had a very high work ethic and were very critical of his performance unless it met their standards. He knew that if he slacked off, his parents would be quick to point out where he needed to improve. To avoid criticism and earn praise, he learned to do everything to a high standard. What is more, George believed that the high standard should apply to those with whom he associated as well.

It worked in grade school where he could earn grades.

It worked as a university student with his mentor where he could gain favors. It worked as a KGB officer where rules provided strict guidelines of behavior.

This attitude did not work so well once he found himself in environments with no structure and rules. George liked plans and didn't trust his gut reaction when confronted with an unpredictable situation, so he became rigid and dogmatic in his thinking and actions.

CONSTRUCTING GEORGE'S PERSONALITY PROFILE

Our birth is but a sleep and a forgetting:
The Soul that rises with us, our life's Star,
Hath had elsewhere its setting,
And cometh from afar:
Not in entire forgetfulness,
And not in utter nakedness,
But trailing clouds of glory do we come
From God, who is our home:
Heaven lies about us in our infancy!
Shades of the prison-house begin to close
Upon the growing Boy,
But He beholds the light, and whence it flows,
He sees it in his joy ...
Mighty Prophet! Seer blest!
Full soon thy Soul shall have her earthly freight,
And custom lie upon thee with a weight,
Heavy as frost, and deep almost as life!
—WILLIAM WORDSWORTH *ODE TO IMMORTALITY*

I spent a great deal of my twenties blaming my parents for what I didn't like about myself. In my thirties, I decided it was time to visit a psychologist and discuss the undesirable personality traits and characteristics I could neither shed nor understand. I walked into my therapist's office with a pen and notebook, convinced that once I told my story, he could give me the answers I needed to move forward.

My therapist's name was Mark. He listened to my story. But instead of providing answers, he only asked questions—most of them about my childhood. I thought, "Oh no, back to the childhood stuff." This is not what I had expected. When I told him about growing up on a cattle ranch, he only asked more questions. I had no idea if my answers were the right ones because he gave me no feedback. As I sat there for an hour, I realized Mark expected me to do all the work!

The Wordsworth poem that I quoted above eloquently explains how children cope with the pressures of life. We do not choose to be born and we do not choose our parents. But we do choose how we shall live and we decide what makes us significant or insignificant. The questions that Mark asked were ones I could ask myself and I didn't have to pay big bucks to do it, either. I felt quite comfortable hacking into other people's lives, but I realized that I needed to start hacking into my own.

I am not against therapists and counselors. I believe people can benefit from gaining more insight into their personality. However, Mark taught me that the hard digging will always be up to me because it is my life.

I've seen how lack of self-awareness allows
people to be manipulated, by people like me

who take the time to understand them better than they understand themselves.

As case agent, my job was to recognize George's personality traits and interpret those behaviors to construct a profile. It led me to look at a variety of theories and approaches, including Myers-Briggs Type Indicator (MCTI) personality test and the Enneagram. I prefer working with the Enneagram because it provides filters that are very easy to understand when interpreting present behavior and predicting future responses.

The Enneagram is comprised of nine personality types and they are divided into three groups of basic human psyche: instinct, feeling, and thinking.[2] The Enneagram is an excellent navigation system to uncover motivations and beliefs that drive behavior.

Each of us exhibits characteristics of all nine personality types, but there will be one type in which our ego and self-image is deeply rooted. There is no such thing as a perfect personality and the purpose of understanding our personality type is not to help us change it or get rid of it. In fact, just the opposite is true. Our basic personalities do not change with age or circumstances. Within each personality type, there are different behaviors that manifest when we are stressed and when we are relaxed.

When we get in touch with our personality, it becomes more transparent and enables us to live to our fullest potential. We are awakened and empowered to live with authenticity, purpose, and a strong mind.

"The Bible says that a deep sleep fell upon Adam, and nowhere is there a reference to his waking up."
—A COURSE IN MIRACLES

A lot of information about the Enneagram can be found on the Internet. There are many on-line tests you can take to more clearly identify your personality type. In addition, it's a good idea to work with a coach who understands how personality type influences our behavior and beliefs. In her book *InsideOut Enneagram: The Game-Changing Guide for Leaders,* Wendy Appel explains how the filters through which you see yourself in the world will shape your response to life.

While not exhaustive, below is the Enneagram's summary of the nine common personality traits from childhood you carry within you. You bring your history into each new moment, giving it meaning and perspective that is uniquely your own. Identify your personality type to help you understand how your fears and desires influence your behavior.

FEELING GROUP

The Feeling Group in the Enneagram is past-oriented because our self-image is built up out of memories and interpretations of the past. This group of personalities seldom dares to be in our hearts. We substitute all sorts of behavior to avoid real feelings. This is important to understand, however, because at our deepest level, our heart qualities are the source of our identity. When our hearts are open, we know who and what we are.

Within the Feeling Group, there are several personality types, and I have listed their traits. If you recognize yourself, there are some tactics I suggest you try to expand your self-awareness.

PEOPLE PLEASER

"I have found the paradox, that if you love until it hurts, there can be no more hurt, only more love."
—MOTHER THERESA

Childhood Fear: Being unloved and unwanted.
Characteristics: Known to be generous, good at building relationships, warm, caring, empathic, doing for others to get love, appreciation, and approval.
Warning Signs: Please others to get approval. Seduce people into caring about you. Make yourself indispensable. Play the martyr. Induce guilt. Manipulator.
Motto: I support and empower others; they couldn't do it without me.
Examples: Mother Theresa, Ann Landers, and Eleanor Roosevelt
Thinking Trap: I can support and empower those around me. I'll be OK as long as I'm working with people.
Positive: I am a generous leader who brings out the best in my employees.
Negative: I can be prideful and a martyr.

TACTICS:

Recall a time when you felt compelled to help someone. What was your motivation?

What does helping others look like to you?

When you try to please someone, do you have an expectation of getting something in return?

What activity or action pushes you toward the unknown?

What does love look like? What does it feel like?

OVER-ACHIEVER

"Winning isn't everything. It's the only thing."
—VINCE LOMBARDI

Childhood Fear: Being worthless and without value apart from their achievements.

Characteristics: Known as over-achievers and workaholics. Competing to be the best at everything and will take short-cuts to get to the goal. Charismatic, charming, optimistic, and adaptable.

Warning Signs: Must be the best in all you do. If you can't be assured of success, you won't take on the challenge. Ignore relationships—goals are more important. Others are there to make you look good. Obsessed with image and success.

Motto: The world is a contest I can win if I work hard and appear successful.

Examples: Donald Trump, Oprah Winfrey, and Bill Clinton

Thinking Trap: I need to be seen based on my achievements. I'll be OK if the environment is fast moving, competitive, and entrepreneurial.

Positive: I am goal-oriented, enthusiastic, and an over-achiever.

Negative: I am deceitful and a workaholic.

TACTICS:

Think about a time when you felt the need to achieve your goal at all costs. What triggered your need?

How have you repeated this pattern in your life?

What has been the cost to you?

How have you been deeply touched?

What activity or action pushes you toward the unknown?

What does achievement look like? What does it feel like?

INDIVIDUALIST

"It is better to drink of deep griefs than to taste shallow pleasures."

—WILLIAM HAZLITT

Childhood Fear: Having no personal significance.

Characteristics: Known as dramatic and expressive but also determined to be authentic and unique. You are self-aware, sensitive, and driven by quality and style.

Warning Signs: Perceive oneself as a victim, happiness is not meant for you. Focus on what is missing, create drama to get attention, the ordinary is mundane. It's OK to be temperamental, moody, melancholy, and sad.

Motto: I am unique and my work has grace, style, and authenticity.

Examples: Judy Garland, Elizabeth Taylor, and Stanley Marcus

Thinking Trap: I like to explore my creativity and deep feelings. I'll be OK if I'm true to myself.

Positive: I am sensitive and refined and I get to the heart of the matter.

Negative: I am envious, often depressed, and impossible to please.

TACTICS:

When have you experienced envy?

What triggered this need or compulsion?

How has this pattern played out in your life?

How often do you focus your attention to what is missing in your life?

What activity or action pushes you toward the unknown?

What does being true to yourself look like? What does it feel like?

THINKING GROUP

The Thinking Group is concerned about the future. We are more apt to ask, "What is going to happen to me?" "How can I survive?" "How do I cope?" This group cannot get our minds to simmer down. We seldom have access to the quiet, spacious qualities of the mind. Instead, our mind is a constant chatterbox, forever trying to come up with strategies or formulas that will allow us to function better in the world.

Here are the personality types and tactics.

OBSERVER

"Knowledge is power."

—FRANCIS BACON

Childhood Fear: Being incompetent, unprepared, and helpless.
Characteristics: Known as intellects, innovative, insightful, and experts who surround themselves with knowledgeable people. They are also isolated, detached, and crave predictability.
Warning Signs: Your expertise is your true source of power. Don't show emotion and don't let people affect you. Withdraw from reality into your concepts of reality. Tend to be introverts.
Motto: My world is built around knowledge.
Examples: Bill Gates, Al Gore, and Howard Hughes
Thinking Trap: I will succeed by gathering all the information available. I'll be OK as long as I can work alone and have few demands for interpersonal relationships.

Positive: I am analytical, a self-starter, and respectful.

Negative: I can be arrogant and a loner.

TACTICS:

Recall a time when you needed to be alone and detach from others. What triggered this need?

How has this pattern played out in your life?

What has been the cost to you?

Recall a time when you made contact with your heart. What were the circumstances?

What activity or action pushes you toward the unknown?

What does being competent look like? What does it feel like?

LOYALIST

"You gain strength, courage, and confidence by every experience in which you really stop to look fear in the face."

—ELEANOR ROOSEVELT

Childhood Fear: Being vulnerable and not being able to survive on their own.

Characteristics: Known as having excellent follow-through, responsible, prepared, team player, champion of colleagues and friends but also anxious and suspicious of the motives of others.

Warning Signs: Anticipate what could go wrong and focus on potential obstacles because you need to know. Don't listen to your intuition. Magnify the negative. Always asking, What if …?

Motto: The world is dangerous, appearances are deceptive, and I need allies.

Examples: Woody Allen, Sigmund Freud, and Richard Nixon

Thinking Trap: I worry about lack of support or guidance and of being unable to succeed on my own. I'll be OK if I can prepare, proceed with caution, and question constantly.

Positive: I am a builder of coalitions and a great team player.

Negative: I can be a skeptic and immobilized by fear.

TACTICS:

Write down a time when you had deep faith and trust in yourself. What were the circumstances?

How can you re-create those same circumstances in your life now?

What are you most afraid of?

What enables you to be courageous?

What activity or action pushes you toward the unknown?

What does being courageous look like? What does it feel like?

ENTHUSIAST

> *"The pessimist sees the difficulty in every opportunity; an optimist sees the opportunity in every difficulty."*
> —WINSTON CHURCHILL

Childhood Fear: Being bored, unhappy, and unable to find fulfillment.

Characteristics: Known as spontaneous, spirited, visionaries who are always looking to the future. They often leave closure to others because they're off on another project. Curious, optimists, upbeat, and playful.

Warning Signs: Believing there is something better out there. Making too many plans and taking on too many projects. Always keeping your options open. Not completing what you've started. Running away from feelings and being overwhelmed. You can be impulsive and scattered.

Motto: The world is full of exciting possibilities; my mission is to explore them.

Examples: Richard Branson, Steve Jobs, and Goldie Hawn

Thinking Trap: I don't want to miss out on anything in life. I'll be OK if I can always be happy.

Positive: I am a visionary, fun and imaginative.

Negative: I can be a glutton and a scatterbrain.

TACTICS:

Recall a time when you've felt trapped by a relationship or situation. What were you afraid might happen?

What triggered your fear?

How does this pattern play out in your life?

How do your dreams in life reflect your vision for the future?

What activity or action pushes you toward the unknown?

What does happiness look like? What does it feel like?

INSTINCT GROUP

While our minds and feelings can wander to the past or the future, our body and gut instinct exists only here and now. The Instinct Group is acutely aware of the internal tensions that reside within us. We live in the present and attempt to use our will to affect the world around us because we don't want to be affected by our environment. We also have more problems with aggression than either the Thinking Group or the Feeling Group, although each personality type deals with it in different ways: Challengers tend to act out of rage, Peacemakers tend to deny it, and Perfectionists tend to repress it.

CHALLENGER

> *"It is fatal to enter any war without the will to win it."*
> —DOUGLAS MACARTHUR

Childhood Fear: Being controlled by others.

Characteristics: Known as self-confident, liking challenges, direct, expressive, big risk takers, strategic, powerful, and take charge. You are also willful and confrontational.

Warning Signs: Using more power and force than necessary. Zero tolerance for subtlety. Blunt and no-nonsense. Shout first, ask questions later. Contempt for rules and laws. Confront and intimidate—don't worry about the consequences. Tend to be extroverts.

Motto: I am strong and in charge.

Examples: Saddam Hussein, John Wayne, and Lyndon Johnson

Thinking Trap: I like environments that are high risk, high engagement, and high energy. I'll be OK as long I can engage immediately and get a lay of the land.

Positive: I have a take-charge attitude and make decisive decisions.

Negative: I can be lustful, bossy, insensitive, and confrontational.

> **TACTICS:**
>
> Recall a time when you felt controlled by another person or situation. What was your reaction?
>
> How has this pattern played out in your life?
>
> Remember a time when you acted on impulse and then justified your actions. What was going on in your thought process at the time?
>
> How has this pattern served you well in life?
>
> What activity or action pushes you toward the unknown?
>
> What does being in control look like? What does it feel like?

PEACEMAKER

> *"Because of indifference, one dies before one actually dies."*
>
> —ELIE WIESEL

Childhood Fear: Fear of conflict.
Characteristics: Known as peacemakers, healers, good implementers, and a stabilizing influence.

Warning Signs: Avoid conflict. Don't share needs, desires, or opinions. Indifferent, resistant to change, complacent, and passive.

Motto: Everything will work out if we stay calm and connected.

Examples: Ronald Reagan, Julia Child, and Jerry Seinfeld

Thinking Trap: I'm concerned about getting lost and swallowed up. I'll be OK if there is a stable and predictable environment with a clear delineation of responsibilities.

Positive: I am empathic, reliable, warm, and the salt of the earth.

Negative: I can be slothful and resistant to change.

TACTICS:

Think of a time that you remained indifferent to a situation rather than address it. What caused you to seek comfort rather than confront the situation?

How does this pattern play out in your life?

How do you disappear into your inner world of peace?

How do you fulfill your dreams in life?

What activity or action pushes you toward the unknown?

What does being passive look like? What does it feel like?

PERFECTIONIST

> *"Whenever you aim for perfection, you find it's a moving target."*
>
> — GEOFFREY FISHER

Childhood Fear: Being wrong and not having integrity.

Characteristics: Known to be an idealist with integrity, self-control, social graces, high standard of behavior. Always looking to do things right, continual self-improvement, and continual focus on how to improve people, processes, and situations.

Warning Signs: You are your inner critic. You are the final arbitrator of right and wrong. Something is not right and you need to fix it. There is always room for improvement. Enjoy your life later; there is always work to be done. You have repressed anger, and festering resentments.

Motto: There is a right way, and let me show you.

Examples: Hillary Clinton, Martha Stewart, and Margaret Thatcher

Thinking Trap: I want to be seen as someone with integrity. I'll be OK if things are in order, I have a clear objective in my work, and there is respect for standards.

Positive: I am principled, scrupulous, and noble.

Negative: I am judgmental, self-righteous, and unforgiving.

TACTICS:

Recall a time when you felt the need to be right. What triggered this need?

How does this pattern play out in your life?

How do you express dissatisfaction or anger with others?

How has this worked for you?

What has been the cost to you?

What activity or action pushes you toward the unknown?

What does perfection look like? What does it feel like?

Do any of these traits feel more pronounced than others? You will experience all of these desires and fears at some point in your life, but one of them will be the dominant lens through which you view life. If you let it, it will place a limit on you and keep you confined in a very small box with little room to grow. It takes courage to break through the barriers that defined you since childhood.

When confronted with a new situation, pay attention to your first response. Once you do, you'll be able to spot trends. The thing to remember is that all responses have a positive and negative aspect to them so there is no such thing as a perfect personality.

Don't live in the past, but it's a great place to visit. Looking back, for most people, is usually a mixed bag. There are bright moments, but there are also shadows. To truly understand ourselves, however, we need to look at both the light and the shadow.

The past gives us a footprint of behavior. It isn't always clear at the time, but in retrospect, there are patterns. We can see our story from a spiritual, as well as emotional, point of view. Our past patterns of behavior make it easier to predict how we'll react to similar situations in the future.

INTERPRETING GEORGE'S PERSONALITY PROFILE

I began identifying with George.

When I was young, I was taught that it was extremely important to perform well on a horse. We had no hired help so it was just my Dad, brother, and myself to gather, herd, and trail hundreds of head of cattle on our Wyoming ranch of several thousands of acres. My parents were pragmatic people and I was not encouraged to express my own feelings. The cattle, horses, and ranch took priority because they provided our income. I developed the habit of suppressing my feelings, and instead, focused on doing a good job and getting top marks in school. These beliefs and behavior, which led to acceptance and love as a child, stayed with me throughout my adult life.

My self-image was connected to:

Setting goals and achieving them.
Denying feelings and focusing on performance.
Believing I would be loved if I performed well.

When George was young, fear of his parent's disapproval for doing something wrong affected the way in which he viewed himself. He was his worst inner critic. He became a workaholic because he was raised to believe there was always room for improvement in his performance. There was a lot of repressed anger and resentment, especially toward others who did not work as hard as he did.

George's self-image was connected to:

Being scrupulous and principled.
Having high standards and always looking to do things right.
Believing he would be loved for doing things the right way.

George was a Perfectionist personality type on the Enneagram. The new intelligence service under Russian President Vladimir Putin was not the same KGB George had joined back in the early 1980's. He felt a lack of integrity on the part of his government. His childhood had trained him to appreciate structure and rules, and he felt both were crumbling under the KGB's successor, the FSB.

His childhood had trained him to be a perfectionist, and perfectionists tend to be judgmental of others. George was no exception; he felt his FSB comrades were badly trained and lacking in professionalism.

George's dream was to be seen as important and powerful. He would never consider openly defecting to the United States. I knew that any overt FBI approach must provide a way for him to see himself as principled and full of integrity. Acknowledgment by the FBI hierarchy of management would be important to him. George would feel comfortable with the controlled order that comes from a good bureaucracy. Without this vital information, we would never been able to make the next move in our investigation. Our approach to George was similar to a business deal, steeped in rigid structure and presented as an opportunity to "do the right thing" with respect to his personal values. We presented him with an offer that allowed him to save face and yet continue to provide us with information of positive intelligence value.

The FBI worked on George's case for several years. Our approach to him had to be carefully constructed because he had such strict boundaries of acceptable behavior. The UCA's job was to provide us with the information needed to construct our personality profile. The trust and bond developed between the UCA and George was legitimate; George never learned of the true identity of the UCA.

I never met George even though I was the case agent. He would not respond favorably to a woman being in a position of power over him, so I swallowed my pride and handed the interview over to an older male agent.

George did accept our offer.

THINKING ABOUT INNER VISION

Point to Ponder: The filters through which you see yourself in the world will shape your response to life.

Inspiration: *"Be careful how you think; your life is shaped by your thoughts."*—Proverbs 4:23

Reflection Question: What trends in my behavior have I noticed in myself?

SELF-AWARENESS

"Your visions will become clear only when you can look into your own heart. Who looks outside, dreams; who looks inside, awakes."

—CARL JUNG

The quickest way to get fired as an FBI agent is to lie. Proven lack of candor is automatic dismissal—truth is a precious commodity in an organization whose primary purpose is peeling back layers of deceit to expose cold, hard facts.

Many of us have a love/hate relationship with truth. We tell ourselves we want to know the truth but we're very selective about the kind of truth we seek. About others, yes—and usually about world events and situations that impact us directly, but we are less receptive to revelations about ourselves.

In fact, the truth about ourselves can be a two-edged sword because we might find out something we would rather not know. We've carefully packaged ourselves to look and act in a manner that ensures success in the world. Our ego has dressed us up for so long that many of us don't even know how to begin to peel back the layers of illusion to expose cold, hard facts about ourselves.

The Book of LaRae was quite short for many years. I, like many others, spent most of my life acting out the role and living up to the identity I'd given myself. There was little of substance because I hadn't taken the time to excavate the significance of my own stories and experiences. I had the form, but little else.

This is ironic because peeling back the layers to get at the truth was my job. Yet I had never applied the same science to my own life. As a counterintelligence FBI agent, I identified foreign spies operating in the United States and tried to persuade them to work for the FBI. Identifying them was the easy part; I surrounded them with undercover agents or informants who insinuated themselves into the spy's life. They then reported the activities of the spy back to me on a regular basis. I could also set up covert surveillance and have agents and trained FBI personnel follow them to alert me of clandestine meetings. Finally, wiretaps are always a good way to get information on a person I was investigating.

A successful recruitment of a foreign spy, however, means digging deep and uncovering what gives their life meaning. Movies and television imply blackmail and extortion are the most effective way to gain the cooperation of a foreign spy or traitor, but this isn't true. These methods work one time, but are rarely fruitful in the long term. Instead, by empowering the targets of my investigations to be truthful about their dreams and goals in life, I empowered them to change direction so they would be moving toward something that had more meaning for them.

When did the Book of LaRae start to thicken up?

George's recruitment operation was one of the most successful cases I had ever worked. One of the reasons it was so successful was the personality profile we had been able to assemble, thanks in large part to the close relationship of the UCA and his invaluable input. I mentioned earlier that I began to identify with George. I saw the impact that his background and childhood had on his behavior and beliefs. We were both driven by our personality type to accomplish our goals in life, albeit our motives were very different. As a perfectionist, George felt the need to do things the right way; as an achiever, I felt the need to do things to get attention. This knowledge is empowering.

PREDICT THE FUTURE

"He who knows others is learned; he who knows himself is wise."

—LAO TZU

Do not fear the future; instead, read the past.

As an FBI agent, I've spent most of my adult life learning how to move into the unknown. By spotting trends in my own past behavior, I know that I'm one of those achievers who look at the world as something to conquer—a contest I can win. I get bored easily and I like things to move fast. This self-knowledge provides me with critical information when I try to predict my future responses to situations and my relationships with other people.

The more I pay attention to my behavior, the better I can predict it. The only person who can change my situation is me. If I ever stop believing this, I've pulled the covers over my head and given up.

GEORGE'S MISTAKE

Don't grow old, grow better.

We need to grow to be our best, and although growing can be both painful and awkward at times, it is the one thing that we must do for ourselves. Personal empowerment allows us to tap into the power that lies within us. We do this by letting go of what doesn't work for us.

George did not understand what wasn't working for him because he had not stopped to reflect upon his career situation for what it truly was. He believed that it would turn into something different in the future, but the crucial element was the fact that George had not taken the time to understand why his life with the KGB was no longer working for him. George was not self-aware, so was unable to see where self-limiting beliefs had derailed his path when he wasn't paying attention. Only George could take responsibility for getting to where he was in life, and if he was disappointed in what he found, take responsibility for staying stuck as long as he had already.

As George begin to think about what was keeping him tethered to his current situation, he needed to become aware of how self-limiting beliefs floated around in his unconscious and limited his performance.

He did not notice them until confronted with a volatile environment that required him to continually adapt to stressful circumstances. George was out of his comfort zone and he did not see a way out of his situation.

Until the FBI provided him with one.

MISSING THE BIG PICTURE OF LIFE

Listen to your own wisdom.

I can size up a person with just a glance and it doesn't take FBI training. So can you, because humans have an amazing capacity to process complex information. Our brain's ability to bring order out of chaos and place people, words, and behavior into patterns that make sense can also work against us. Below is a paragraph[3] that raced across the Internet a few years back:

"Aoccdrnig to a rscheearch at Cmabrigde Uinervtisy, it deosn't mttaer in waht oredr the ltteers in a wrod are, the olny iprmoetnt tihng is taht the frist and lsat ltteer be at the rghit pclae. The rset can be a toatl mses and you can sitll raed it wouthit porbelm. Tihs is bcuseae the huamn mnid deos not raed ervey lteter by istlef, but the wrod as a wlohe."

This valuable ability to seek out patterns is an excellent example of how our focus on the "big picture" can leave us missing important details. Our intellectual strength represents a liability when it leads us to miss something that we might have otherwise noticed. It can be a built-in limitation if we're not aware of it.

Here are ways I learned to become more self-aware.

Eavesdrop on Yourself. Take the time to notice what is working in your life, and what is not.

Our training at the FBI Academy hammered in the importance of situational awareness. It is not just FBI agents who need to be constantly aware of their surroundings. You and I experience changes in our environment all the time. Most of these changes are not volatile or hostile, but you can train yourself to be alert so that if you are confronted with a situation that demands a quick decision, you will feel prepared to make the right one.

An excellent way of gaining clarity on how your mind works when confronted with unexpected news or surprising events is to eavesdrop on yourself. Do this by writing down everything that comes to mind as you recollect a recent conversation where you needed to make a quick decision or deal with unexpected news.

If the information was delivered through a conversation, try to get permission from the other person to record it. "I didn't know I said that." "I didn't realize I thought that." These are common reactions when you review your notes or replay the conversation. This is why friends can be great sounding boards. You are able to discover not so much what they think, but instead, what you think as you talk through the issue.

As I became aware of the patterns in my decisions, choices, and habits, I could identify the ones that helped me learn from adversity. Each time I acted out of anger, I strengthened my mind's anger response; the only way I could stop the negative pattern of behavior was to recognize anger as an emotion that caused me to move away from one of my values. Anger dulled my ability to think rationally and objectively, and when this happened, I didn't tap into my intelligence (one of my personal values) to help me make a better decision.

Similarly, when I am honest, it strengthens my mind's integrity response. I moved toward my value of integrity. Self-awareness is getting to know the important details about your own life.

Surveillance. If an FBI agent wants to know more about a person, the first thing we do is put the individual under surveillance. It is the simplest, most direct way to collect information about another person. Surveillance can provide loads of data on a person's habits, values, choices, hobbies, dreams, and goals.

I encourage you to place yourself under surveillance as well. You can do this quite easily by keeping a journal. Writing in a journal is sitting down and opening a vein.

Journaling can help you tap into your subconscious and your own inner wisdom. This is where you will find your authentic voice—the one who knows who you really are, what you want, and how to get there.

Journaling can be a scary process for some because it will expose your vulnerabilities as it peels back layers of your personality. It has been a truly transformative process for me and I know it has been for many others as well. One of the reasons that journaling is so effective is that it forces you to slow down and become more grounded. You get so busy with life that you can no longer hear that inner voice. You still have the answers to your own questions, but you don't slow down enough for that voice to be heard.

I have specific requirements for my journal. I buy flat bound notebooks that are thin so my hand rests well when writing. I don't like ringed notebooks that impede handwriting across either page. I do not use computer journals because the act of writing helps me to disentangle my thoughts. I allow myself to wrestle through issues, process events, and interpret conversations. This helps me to understand the context in which these things are happening in my life. Life happens so quickly that, unless I journal, I don't take the time to stop and reflect on where I'm heading.

Spontaneous Responses. Listen to the words of your experience. As an FBI agent, I've been taught to pay particular attention to gut reactions. These are the responses that are unfiltered and often reveal the strongest mental and emotional connections.

> When I ask a question, the first response the interviewee blurts out is usually the most accurate in revealing their true feelings on an issue.

When they have time to think about it, they often to try modifying their reaction so it looks, feels, and sounds more compatible to the image they have of themselves, or the one they want me to have of them.

When interviewing subjects suspected of a crime, these are examples of gut reactions that almost always indicate deception:

"What could happen to a person who did that?"

"I wouldn't do anything like that."

"NO, absolutely NOT. It could not have been me."

"It could have been the person who sits next to me."

"Don't hurt me."

Criminals are not the only ones who tell others about themselves through their spontaneous responses. Ordinary people reveal themselves under stress, and daily life offers hundreds of opportunities to uncover revealing insight into your own personality. Pay attention to your first reaction when you receive news or need to make a decision. For example you ask a colleague to stay late and help you on a project with a deadline. They respond, "I'm leaving a little early today so I can spend more time with my kids." What is your gut response?

Do you smile with understanding and feelings of warmth? Are you suspicious and assume the kids are an excuse? Do you wonder how the person will ever get ahead by putting the job second? As you process these reactions, they may change but the initial response is always the one that runs truest and most accurately reveals your dominant traits.

For example, if you responded with a smile and feelings of warmth, your first inclination is that of a people-person. Relationships are important to you. If you responded with suspicion that the kids were just an excuse, you'd make a great FBI agent because you're a skeptic. And if you wondered how they would ever get ahead, you're the achiever type who believes in order to get ahead in life you need to put your shoulder into it.

Spontaneous reactions expose approval or disapproval of the tasks that you're dealing with as well. If your first reaction is one of excitement and anticipation, chances are good that you're engaged in something that is meaningful to you. Pay attention to your initial reactions to people, projects, events, and situations. They can be important clues to help you develop more self-awareness.

Self-awareness is the cornerstone of a strong mind. This book shares part of my journey with you. I chose the topics of authenticity, purpose, courage, confidence, determination, and resilience as the path to a strong mind because this is how my self-awareness of a strong mind unfolded for me.

THINKING ABOUT SELF-AWARENESS

Point to Ponder: As you strive to be more authentic in the way you live your life, you must also cultivate a high degree of self-awareness.

Inspiration: *"Leaders with self-awareness understand they don't just exchange information, they influence people's moods and emotions."*—Steve Gutzler

Reflection Question: What has shaped me into the person I am today?

AUTHENTICITY TACTICS

I am an investigator by training so one of the very first things I learned is that while theories are nice, data is better. As I mentioned in the Introduction, I am going to ask that you do your own sleuthing and make yourself the subject of your own investigation. The TACTICS will ask you to pay attention to what is going on in your life now, recall what has gone on in the past, and where you want to go in the future. These are not opportunities to beat yourself up for mistakes or weaknesses. But before something can change, you need to fully identify it.

Collect data to find out what is true and what works for you. I believe the best way to improve your chances at success is to see how and why you are not successful in areas that are important to you. Self-knowledge is the foundation of leadership and empowerment.

Remember, the TACTICS are optional. If they do not speak to you now, feel free to give them a pass.

VALUES

Here are some questions that will help you identify your top values in life:

What are the three things I like most and least about myself?

_____

Who is the happiest person I know?

_____

Who are the two people I like and respect the most and why?

_____

Who Am I?

_____

What is most important to me in life?

_____

This is a partial list of values—see how many more you can add:

    Integrity
    Patience
    Honesty
    Gratitude
    Humility
    Forgiveness

Compassion *Importantly*

Passion *Empathy*

Love *Respectful*

Freedom

Happiness *caring*

Fun *Living*

Intelligence *Proudness*

Perseverance *Considerate*

Spirituality

Joy

Family

Relationships

Health

Wealth

Education

Adventure

Creativity

Career

Ubuntu's

List your **TOP FIVE** values. Identifying your top five values is a shortcut to identifying your top goals in life.

1. _____

2. _____

3. _____

4. _____

5. _____

SELF-AWARENESS

If you are still uncertain how to dig deeper into self-awareness, here are other areas to think about:

Power: Identify when you've used your power and influence in ways that have enhanced your leadership of others.

Achievement: List your successes. Did you acknowledge those who helped you to succeed?

Self-Gratification: Remember the times you've enjoyed your life and felt pleasure in giving to others.

Motivation: Who inspires you? Why? Who do you inspire?   ∠12 M·y·J

Self-Direction: Celebrate the times you've been curious enough about yourself that you stopped in your busy schedule to find out more.

Benevolence: Remember the times you've treated others with a spirit of honesty, helpfulness, forgiveness, loyalty, and friendship. Commit to doing it more often.

Tradition: Pinpoint the instances when you've reacted with humbleness and respect.

Conformity: Notice your self-discipline (or lack of) when confronted with the unexpected, disappointment, and adversity.

Security: Remind yourself that you are not an island and not alone. How have you rejoiced in belonging to something bigger than yourself? *Relyn*

Spirituality: Remember the times you felt God's hand on your shoulder giving you guidance and strength.

Connect

Strong minds are capable of making decisions in challenging and stressful environments because their choices are based on their values. They understand themselves well enough that they can predict their behavior when faced with adversity. Authenticity is the desire to be real. Genuine—not an imitation. To get to authenticity you will need to keep digging to uncover who you are and what you believe. To discover the inevitability of where your life is taking you, you must find purpose.

CHAPTER 2
PURPOSE

"The man without purpose is like a ship without a rudder—a waif, a nothing, a no man."

—THOMAS CARLYLE

The national media dubbed 1985 the Year of the Spy because it was the year in which the FBI arrested eight foreign spies operating on American soil. Most of them were operatives of Communist countries and tensions were high as Mikhail Gorbachev and Ronald Reagan discussed the future of the Cold War that same year.

Two years later, I was transferred to the FBI's San Francisco office where the Silicon Valley was putting Northern California on the map as the mother lode of cutting edge technology, including U.S. military and defense projects. I was assigned to a counterintelligence squad and given my first assignment working as an undercover agent against the Soviets.

The year was 1987, before the fall of the Soviet Union. My job was to identify a KGB officer who was expected to travel with a large Soviet trade delegation that would be visiting an American company in the Silicon Valley. This same company was also working on a classified nano-technology defense project.

The KGB was a creature of habit and always inserted one of its officers into these types of high-level delegations—particularly this one since the host company was also involved in classified military research. The FBI had no leads as to the identity of the KGB officer so I had very little to help narrowing down the field of possible suspects.

> One thing I did know was that the officer would not be a female. In those days, the KGB did not train women as officers; they might be recruited as an operative or an agent but weren't allowed the same status as an officer.

My assignment was to figure out which person among the delegation of thirty-six scientists and managers was working for the KGB. I represented myself as an individual working for an international public relations company. A legitimate PR firm had provided backstopping, which meant they were willing to vouch for me as one of their contract employees. I had taken several journalism classes while working on my Masters in communication at Arizona State University, so I used this background to establish credibility. Further, I leaned into my prior experience in retail management for my cover story. I told people I had worked in public relations for a large department store chain but this was my first job working for a PR firm. My relative youth (I was in my late twenties) excused my lack of professional experience but I came across as eager and ambitious—perfect combination for PR. I never veered far from my real life story, including my upbringing on a cattle ranch in Wyoming.

While I knew I could come across as authentic in my undercover role, I was less confident on how to accomplish my mission. I felt powerless, in over my head, and lacked confidence.

> I had been through undercover training at the FBI Academy in Quantico, Virginia but I had no idea how to find this guy. It was scary—very scary for me because the stakes were so high. The Soviets were trying to steal classified military technology and my job was to protect the security of the United States.

Dressed conservatively, I attended receptions and conferences and got to know the delegates. They spoke English, so language was no problem. I spent most of my time observing the behavior and body language of each delegate rather than trying to impress them with my knowledge of PR.

I moved around the room during the lectures and subsequent social breaks to get closer to different members of the Soviet delegation so I could observe them or possibly overhear their conversations with Americans. The Soviets were easy to spot—cheap and wrinkled suits, generic black shoes with thick black soles, and chopped haircuts. When they sat together, they spoke Russian. I don't speak the language and didn't know what they were saying, although their conversation was punctuated by lots of laughter and backslapping.

So I approached them individually and spoke in English. All were polite and willing to engage in conversation, but once they knew I was in public relations, their eyes started darting around the room for someone more important to engage. No genuine scientist is interested in learning more about how PR works.

Interestingly, as I got to know each "suspect," one of them did stand out. He wasn't the one who asked the most questions. He wasn't the pushy one trying to get cozy with the top American scientists or the big, ugly one who looked like a KGB goon. The man who came to my attention was the one who clearly was not passionate about nano-technology.

He was the only member of the Soviet delegation who did not take notes during lectures. Instead, it looked as though he was drawing on his notebook paper. He never asked questions after a lecture and rarely approached the experts at receptions. I even found him reading a book written in Russian during the lunch hour instead of networking like all the other Soviet delegates.

As a new agent, without knowing how, I had accurately identified this man, Nicholas (not his real name) as the KGB officer assigned to accompany the delegation. I told the case agent that I was suspicious of Nicholas because he was the one guy who didn't want to be there. Once the FBI had Nicholas in their sights, we sent requests for full identification to Interpol, international intelligence agencies, and the CIA. We picked away until we had identified him for what he truly was—a seasoned intelligence officer who had a distinguished career with the KGB.

Nicholas appeared complacent and showed little interest in the project. At times, he even looked a little bored.

The secret to being a spymaster, first and foremost, is the ability to recognize the truth about people.

The most effective spymasters are those who crack through the armor of a person's personality to reveal the most basic needs and desires we all experience as human beings. Counterintelligence agents like myself are not psychologists, but we are patient observers of human behavior. I sensed that Nicholas's seeming complacency was a symptom of something that ran much deeper.

I looked for a way to introduce myself to him. My opportunity came during a business conference of around two hundred people when the seat next to him was empty. I stepped on the toes of a woman wearing lime green shoes to get to the seat first, apologized, and settled in with an open and friendly face. My habit was to either wear a wedding band or an engagement ring so it would be clear that I had no romantic overtures in mind.

Russian men were not known for being sharp dressers but Nicholas was a bit more sophisticated—his suit pants had a knife-edge crease and his shoelaces looked as though they had been ironed. His English was very good and when he smiled, his teeth were straight and white—not a smoker, I thought.

I brought a paperback book with me, and during the breaks at this conference I sat in my chair and read *Zen and the Art of*

Motorcycle Maintenance. Nicholas immediately noticed the book and asked about it. When I told him it was about self-discovery, he was intrigued and we started talking. The topic turned to how to find a life of meaning and I borrowed a line from Charlotte Gilman: "Life is a verb, not a noun."

That was the beginning of our friendship. I could see by the look in his face that my comment sparked something significant for him. It broke loose a train of thought and action that would soon take his life in a totally different direction.

In later conversations, Nicholas told me he was beginning to question his purpose in life. Like most of us, Nicholas started with asking this question of himself at a young age. "What career should I pursue?" "What are my talents?" These are good questions and need to be answered, but they do not go deeply enough once you begin to question the significance of your own life.

FINDING PURPOSE AND MEANING

Most of us speculate on our purpose in life and take a hit or miss approach. We think that if we keep at something long enough, or if we want it badly enough, we can make it happen. This may be true, but unless we touch upon a purpose that feeds from who we really are—our authentic self—we are doing nothing more than inflating an ego formed in childhood that will need to be continually fed to feel satisfied.

The purpose of life is to discover your gift.

The work of life is to develop it.

The meaning of life is to give it away.

The remainder of this chapter will break down purpose into three areas: dreams, goals, and mission.

THINKING ABOUT PURPOSE

Points to Ponder: A great life responds to a higher calling and purpose.

Inspiration: *"Put your ear down close to your heart and listen hard."*—Anne Sexton

Reflection Question: What is your highest calling?

DREAMS

"Tell me, what is it you plan to do with your one wild and precious life?"

—MARY OLIVER

My conversations with Nicholas around the topics brought up in *Zen and the Art of Motorcycle Maintenance* opened the door for a relationship to develop between us. He was physically fit and liked to do things outdoors so I introduced him to another agent who posed as my boyfriend and the three of us would go hiking in the Santa Cruz Mountains.

Nicholas never brought any water or food but carried a backpack filled to capacity with a camera, tripod, notebook, and nature books. He'd find a spot and set up with his camera, take a few shots, and then spend several minutes writing in his notebook.

I asked him what he was doing and he said he was writing stories for his son—who was about 6 years old. Nicholas said he had seen an American movie called *The Gnome Mobile* when he was a kid and the stories to his son were about "the little people" who lived in the woods.

He had quite an imagination, a great sense of humor, and he could write good fantasy fiction. He would then illustrate the stories, either with the photographs he had taken on our hikes or his own sketches. When I asked him if he planned to publish his children's stories, he said "No." He would like to, but it was just a dream.

THE IMPORTANCE OF DREAMS

His comment made me think of my own childhood. Like most children, I dreamed of a better life.

> I spent a great deal of my early years lacking confidence in my ability to make any of my dreams come true—to have a life of adventure that was not ordinary.

Since I went to a school where there were no other students except my younger brother, I had no friends. The only person I competed against was myself, so it was a continual contest to outdo my own last level of achievement. I can hardly remember a time when I didn't feel the need to be the best in an attempt to gain recognition and acceptance from others.

I knew there was more to experience in life than my narrow world could provide and I yearned to taste something different. I watched Fess Parker on the television series *"Daniel Boone"* and wanted to be like him: a person who embraced adventure, adversity, and challenges. His experiences were exciting because they opened up and uncovered new things about the world around him.

Sometimes the only way I could cope was by shutting down my feelings and pretending nothing else mattered. I dreamed of something bigger, better, and bolder for my life but there was always that warning from adults to "Quit dreaming ... be practical!" It wasn't until I was an adult before I realized that there will *always* be someone to remind us we can't, or shouldn't, or won't. As I became more personally empowered through my experiences and career, I began to understand that I can, should, and will.

I didn't know it when I applied, but the FBI is really a people business. This is what distinguishes the FBI from most other law enforcement agencies around the world. The FBI recruited me as a special agent while I was at Arizona State University working on my Masters in communication. The FBI was on campus for a career day orientation. I was bored with my retail job, and worried that the most significant thing I'd do in my life was persuade women to buy stripes this season instead of polka dots. The thought was depressing—I had not found my purpose in life.

The agent I met with that day on the school campus encouraged me to accomplish more than I ever thought I could, and he pointed out how I'd done more in my life than what I'd given myself credit for. His name was Denny and I'll never forget his black horn-rimmed glasses, white socks, and thick-soled black shoes. He began the interview by asking about where I grew up. He listened intently as I described going to a private school of just my brother and myself because the ranch was so isolated. I couldn't attend a public school but was determined to pursue higher education. He recognized the courage, determination, and resilience needed to move a naïve young country girl into the unknown as I pursued my goals. He also saw the untapped potential that still lay within me. In sum, Denny believed in me more than I believed in myself.

As I got to know Nicholas, the wisdom of my experience told me that I needed to encourage him to live his dream in the same way that Denny had encouraged me to live mine.

FINDING NICHOLAS'S DREAM

Nicholas had stopped believing he could change his future.

He had stopped being the leader of his own life and relied upon a career twenty years old to continue providing him with purpose and direction. My job was to keep Nicholas from stealing vital U.S. defense technology—in FBI jargon, my job was to neutralize him, not be a career counselor. But in order to determine the most effective approach with a spy like Nicholas, it was imperative to gain an understanding of his background and childhood. That provided important information on how his personal values, dreams, and goals were formed. In other words, what made Nicholas tick?

Growing up, the task of taking care of others had always fallen to Nicholas. He was the oldest of six children and it was his job to help his parents to alleviate their stress. He took care of the younger children and there were many times when he felt everyone depended on him to keep the family together. His mom seemed overwhelmed by the stress of her large family so he helped cook and clean. He started working as a street sweeper when he was eleven to help bring in extra income for food and clothes. His father was an unskilled worker who took odd jobs to make ends meet.

Nicholas was a People Pleaser personality type on the Enneagram that I discussed in the previous chapter. Connecting with people was important to him so his way of moving forward was through a loose web of networks with people in different industries, particularly in public relations. They, in turn, knew published authors and literary agents and offered to broker introductions. He didn't need the rigidity of structure and rules. In fact, they intimidated him.

This was a very different approach from George, the Perfectionist personality type. While my ultimate goal was to recruit Nicholas, he would also be neutralized if he were no longer working for a hostile intelligence service.

COMPLACENCY

Complacency will lead to extinction.

As Nicholas and I talked about *Zen and the Art of Motorcycle Maintenance*, it became obvious that he was struggling to understand how to get in touch with his changing goals in life. We started our conversation by talking about his son, but it quickly moved into his own childhood and how difficult it had been to make ends meet. I teased out memories that were significant to him and asked how they impacted his behavior growing up. As a child, it had been important to connect with people in a meaningful way. As an adult, those same needs had been shut down because of the nature of his (covert) job. He never discussed his true assignment in the United States—he was too much of a professional to divulge classified information to anyone.

> **If Nicholas had not been complacent, he would have recognized he was in danger, and not only from me.**

He was unaware of his changing attitude toward his career and how it was no longer fulfilling for him. He became vulnerable because he let his guard down and was no longer alert to the threats that surrounded him and other aspects of his life.

When you become complacent, you're no longer operating from your center, from that place of strength that gives you balance. If you can spot complacency in your behavior or attitude, you know that it's time to re-evaluate your purpose, goals, or vision.

LESSONS ABOUT FRIENDSHIP

One of my favorite quotes by Abraham Lincoln is, "*Am I not destroying my enemies when I make friends of them?*" Nicholas was an enemy agent and I never forgot that. To destroy the enemy did not mean I needed to destroy Nicholas. In fact, helping Nicholas find his purpose in life was obviously moving him away from the Russian intelligence service.

Nicholas was not going to find the purpose of his life inside a book. If he was to be the leader of his own life, he must be willing to look inward to find it. This is often very difficult to do on our own.

> ## We need to surround ourselves with people who care—they create the environment in which we will either thrive or wilt.

If our mind is always open to learning, we can be taught from those who are different or have different values. These are some lessons I learned about friendship and how the right relationships with others can sharpen my mind:

Pick friends wisely. I've come to accept that, in business and life, there will always be people around me who feel that my success will cause them to lose out. I no longer share my dreams and goals with people like them. They may try to undermine me.

I deserve better friends that those who either will not or cannot help me become my best self. Plato once said, "People are like dirt. They can either nourish you and help you grow as a person, or they can stunt your growth and make you wilt and die."

I pick my friends wisely because they create the environment in which I will either succeed for fail. I give everyone the opportunity to be a friend, but I share my dreams and goals only with those who value them as much as I do.

The more I got to know Nicholas, the more I liked him. I genuinely wanted him to be planted in an environment where he could grow to reach his fullest potential. He admitted that his dreams and goals in life had changed over time. We can all identify with

Nicholas because the dreams we had as young adults or in mid-life change as we age, and we need friends who will not only recognize our need to change, but to help us along our path to do so.

Change whom you hang around with. I have had different friends for different parts of my life. When I moved into a different phase of life, I found people who could help me visualize what that future could look like.

Like it or not, we become similar to the friends we hang out with. Our associations have a lot to do with where we're at in every area of our life. Our friends are going to influence our behavior, so why not pick ones who will be a positive influence?

The goal of my undercover operation was to determine if Nicholas could be persuaded to work for the United States. If so, plan the easiest way to introduce an FBI colleague in true name. My undercover identity would not be divulged or compromised.

Even though I used a different first name, it was still possible to build trust. We did this by talking candidly and honestly about our lives, and the things that are important to us. At the beginning of an undercover assignment like this, it's impossible to predict what will be uncovered. I discovered a man whose heart was no longer in his work. I suspected that if Nicholas no longer found fulfillment in his current position with Russian intelligence, he would be no happier working for the FBI doing the same thing.

Establish a benchmark test for choosing friends. I ask myself whether spending time with this person will lift me up or drag me down? Will spending time with this person help me become the person I want to become? Will I be happier after spending time with this person? Will this person help or support me to achieve my most important goals? If not, I will find friends who will.

I learned a lot from Nicholas about being a good friend. He trusted me to help him become his best self. I would have preferred him to agree to working with the FBI, but his goals were loftier because they came from the heart. Not every undercover operation ends in recruiting the foreign spy, but the case would be a success if Nicholas was no longer a threat to the security of the United States.

List five people who can help you achieve your dreams and goals. Make a list of five people whom you trust to listen to you attentively, and tell them about your dreams and goals. Sharing details of our life creates trust, and if you don't feel you can trust a person with the most vulnerable part of yourself—your dream, find someone else for a friend.

People will be vulnerable with you about their higher purpose in life if you are vulnerable with them. Nicholas felt he could trust me because I trusted him first. Conversation revolving around one of these three topics rarely fails to elicit a response.

Job frustration
Relationships
Religion

Sometimes the response is positive, other times it's negative. If I am the first to venture deeper, I am putting myself out there for ridicule, acceptance, or rejection. My comments are honest and from the heart, regardless of the name I'm using that day. Nicholas and I rarely talked about our overt work assignments; instead, we talked about values, childhood memories and scars, dreams, and goals. I, too, had always wanted to be a writer and we talked about how a career in writing would look for each of us.

In the end, Nicholas did not choose to work for the FBI. Instead, he chose to retire early and pursue his dream of writing a children's book. He made the right decision; his dreams, goals and mission in life had changed over time.

THINKING ABOUT DREAMS

Points to Ponder: Give yourself permission to be the person that you choose to be.

Inspiration: *"The only difference between a rut and a coffin are the dimensions."*—Ellen Glasgow

Reflection Question: If you don't have a dream, how can a dream come true?

GOALS

"The tragedy of life does not lie in not reaching your goals; the tragedy of life is in not having any goals to reach. It isn't a calamity to die with dreams unfulfilled, but it is a calamity not to dream. It is not a disaster to be unable to capture your ideal, but it is a disaster to have no ideal to capture. It is not a disgrace not to reach the stars, but it is a disgrace to have no stars to reach for."

—DR. BENJAMIN MAYS

Often, it is our dreams that show us the way toward a future that is full of purpose. The great achievers throughout history began their journey with nothing more than a dream. To make their dreams come true they set goals for themselves.

REVEALING DREAMS IN THE BIBLE

I've told you about Nicholas, and I'll come back to him toward the end of the chapter, but I'd also like to share one of my favorite examples about the significance of dreams, and how a dream led from goals to a mission. The story comes from the Bible's Old Testament. Joseph[4] was a seventeen-year-old Hebrew shepherd who dreamed that one day he would be the boss over his older brothers. His brothers were jealous of him and sold him to a caravan of Ishmaelites for twenty pieces of silver. To explain Joseph's absence, they wiped goat's blood on the coat of many colors that their father had given him and told their father that Joseph had been killed.

Joseph was sold as a slave to Potipher, the captain of the Pharaoh's guard. While serving there, he prospered at everything he did and was promoted to oversee Potipher's entire household. Potipher's wife tried to seduce him, but when he refused, she went to her husband and falsely accused Joseph of rape.

He was thrown into prison, but even there he prospered. The warden put Joseph in charge of the other prisoners. When members of Pharaoh's household were thrown into prison as a temporary punishment for minor offenses, Joseph interpreted their dreams. When they were released, they remembered Joseph's composure, mental toughness, and ability to interpret their dreams. So, when the Pharaoh became troubled by dreams, they recommended Joseph.

He told the Pharaoh that the dreams were foretelling seven years of abundance to be followed by seven years of famine and advised Pharaoh to stock up on grain during the years of abundance. Pharaoh released him from prison, and before Joseph was thirty years of age, he was the highest official over all of Egypt to serve directly under Pharaoh. This story illustrates the powerful possibilities that can be unleashed by a dream.

Joseph had a dream that he would make a difference to the world. To some outsiders, it looked more like a fantasy. Joseph wanted

> this so strongly and thought about it so much
> that he even had dreams about it.

This is why his brothers were so angry. They understood, correctly, that what Joseph spoke of was not merely a dream; it was a clear and strong desire.

Joseph had a strong mind. Many of the qualities that he leaned into as his story unfolded exemplifies how strong minds are formed. Life did not go according to plan for Joseph, and yet he did not flounder when sold into slavery. He learned to not only survive, but to thrive in an environment that was suddenly hostile and volatile.

HAVE A PLAN

Failing to plan is planning to fail.

Joseph knew that failing to have a plan would mean that his dream would fade as many others do. He knew that he would need a clear road map to guide him on the best possible route to follow in achieving his goal. The difference was that he was flexible when plans went awry. Joseph did not plan to be sold into slavery in Egypt by his brothers, but when he was bought as a household servant, he did not give up. He never gave up on his goal, but changed his strategies and tactics to accommodate his new circumstances. He led by remembering his big goal in each situation rather than sticking to a plan that was outdated. Of importance, however, is that once Joseph landed on his feet, he revised his plan and moved forward.

A strong mind draws up a precise plan of action necessary to achieve goals and then gets down to work. A strong mind is also agile, and able to quickly adopt new tactics in hostile and volatile environments. Long-term strategies may also need to be reviewed and revised, depending upon the circumstances.

KEEP GOING WHEN THE GOING GETS TOUGH

Do not abandon your goal when the going gets tough.

Going from the favored son of a wealthy landowner to a household slave in a foreign country calls for leadership in an extreme and isolated environment. He did not give up.

When he became a slave, he gave that position his best shot. Soon, he was recognized as a man of determination and was promoted. For those unfamiliar with the story, in a short time, Joseph climbed the corporate ladder and became the Chief Operating Officer of Egypt. As the story goes, a few years later in a time of famine, his older brothers came to Egypt in search of food and Joseph did rule over them, just as he had dreamed as a youth. It's a great example of how a strong mind survives in a hostile environment and thrives by relying upon the characteristics outlined in this book.

Start focusing on what you need to do to succeed in your current situation and then be the best at it. Do not let yourself think or feel like a victim. Do not abandon your dream and goals because your plans did not initially work out the way you wanted them to.

As a new counterintelligence agent in the FBI, I also had a clear and strong desire because I was doing something I truly enjoyed. I loved my job and I was living my dream. The other option is to experience regret, and regret will cling to your memories more tenaciously than failure.

If we are a strong-minded person like Joseph, we will see failures and obstacles as opportunities to earn a new problem-solving skill. If we discover the worst about ourselves, the discovery will be a new strength. We will think in terms of progress rather than perfection. Finding what we do to be interesting and rewarding is one of the most efficient ways to stay motivated. The learning process will not fatigue us; instead, it will invigorate us. This keeps our eyes on the goals and not on the obstacles or failures.

DESIRE IT

Goals are dreams on paper.

"Your work is going to fill a large part of your life, and the only way to be truly satisfied is to do what you believe is great work. And the only way to do great work is to love what you do. If you haven't found it yet, keep looking. Don't settle. Stay hungry. Stay foolish."

—STEVE JOBS

Research[5] has shown that people who regularly write down their goals earn as much as nine times more than their counterparts who do not write down goals. Over 80% of Americans do not have goals; 16% say they do have goals but don't write them down; less than 4% actually write them down. Guess who they are? They are the ones making nine times more than the rest of us.

Less than 20% of Americans can answer the following questions with any clarity. How would you answer them?

What is my job?

What about my job really counts?

How well am I doing?

Is my job an expression of my personal values?

Can I list my 5 top personal values?

In my job, am I building a life of success, but not of significance?

What can I (or my employer) do to help me become more passionate about my current role?

Is there another job I'd rather be doing?

Why aren't I doing it?

If you cannot find fulfillment in your answers to these questions, chances are good that a silent killer called "rustout" is stalking you. Rustout is more common in America than in other developed countries and it's actually even scarier than "burn-out" because, while burnout can wear down your body, rustout can wipe out your soul and spirit.

"Rustout is the slow death that follows when we stop making the choices that keep life alive. It's the feeling of numbness that comes from taking the safe way, never accepting new challenges, continually surrendering to the day-to-day routine. Rustout means we are no longer growing, but at best, are simply maintaining. It implies that we have traded the sensation of life for the security of a paycheck ... Rustout is the opposite of burnout. Burnout is overdoing ... rustout is underbeing."

—RICHARD LEIDER AND STEVE BUCHHOLTZ, *THE RUSTOUT SYNDROME*

Rustout can be avoided if you set goals for yourself because goals are reminders of the type of person you aspire to be or really are and aspiring to live. They prevent you from dissolving into the gray masses of mediocrity and "underbeing." Those who reach for the higher goal do not suffer from rust out because they are always moving ahead. They have not stalled or retired-in-place, simply allowing the world to continue to move around them.

By looking closely at the example of Joseph, I found an individual committed to reaching for the higher goal. The lessons from his story are as poignant today as they were thousands of years ago.

THINKING ABOUT GOALS

Points to Ponder: Live each day with goals in alignment with your purpose, dreams, and values.

Inspiration: *"If you aim at nothing, you will hit it every time."*— B.J. Marshall

Reflection Question: Over the next five years, what do you really want to do?

MISSION

"Dedicate your life to a cause greater than yourself, and your life will become a glorious romance and adventure."

—MACK DOULAS

As a counterintelligence agent, I uncovered the tender spots of discontent that often lay buried under the noise of life. Once exposed, areas of restlessness often made it possible for me to craft an approach to a foreign spy that would be effective, and usually, unexpected. I found that discontent usually shows up when people are not living according to their true values, or when they are questioning their purpose in life.

When recruiting foreign spies to work for the U.S. government, FBI agents such as myself looked for vulnerabilities in their character. The biggest disruptions in their lives always occurred when they allocated less and less time to the things that mattered most to them.

Nicholas was vulnerable because he was looking to find a deeper meaning in his life and work. Moving him to another assignment would not solve his discontent. A far more productive approach would be to help him find his way out of his current situation and then make an offer for the U.S. Government to subsidize the move to a new career. Our proposal was to pay Nicholas for debriefings regarding his work as a Russian intelligence officer. Nicholas would never officially work for the FBI, but a "data dump" of information can help the FBI counter hostile intelligence activities in the U.S.

A formal arrangement would not appeal to Nicholas. He had no interest in hierarchy or protocol. I brokered introductions to people in the public relations community in the Bay Area. They, in turn, introduced him to consultants who had loose connections with the U.S. Government. These individuals were, in fact, FBI agents. No last names were used and this vague arrangement suited Nicholas very well. The consultants offered to pay Nicholas a handsome sum for debriefings to help finance his new career. He was comfortable with this situation because he was not a person who confronted issues head-on, and this provided him with a layer of deniability for his own safety without openly defying the Russian government.

> Nicholas would have been stronger minded
> if he had bothered to seek out or recognize
> his own vulnerabilities. He was blindsided
> by his own complacency and the frustration
> that often accompanies discontent. He did
> not know that it is important to pay attention
> to his dreams. He was also unaware that
> dreams can shift into clearer focus over time.

I started with my dream—to live an adventurous life that was not ordinary. I turned that dream into a goal—to become an FBI agent. My mission was to bring my personal values into the way

I conducted myself in both business and life. In every investigation, I let these standards of behavior guide my decisions and create a strong mind.

Over the next twenty years, however, I realized that while my dream had not changed, my goals and mission had. Now, my goal was to write and my mission was to encourage others to excavate the significance of their own extraordinary stories and learn from them. A strong mind can be learned, and everyone has the raw resources within their own experiences to create one.

SUCCESS TO SIGNIFICANCE

Your life is worth a noble mission.

The Rolling Stones have taught us a great lesson in life: You can't always get what you want! As the baby boomers hit sixty, many of them are pausing to reflect on this milestone birthday. It is about this time in life when they realize that, while they are no longer young, they still have a lot of life left in them. They begin asking questions like, "When am I going to live my best life? When am I going to do something of significance with my life?"

They spent their younger years raising a family or building a career. Now they have hit the age when they're ready to reckon with their mortality. They are ready to find purpose in their life and make a difference in the world.

Most dictionaries define mission as "a specific task or duty assigned to a group or individual." At some point you will ask yourself this question: What is my mission in life? What is the purpose of my life? Why am I here?

People who are deeply motivated tend to hitch their desire to a cause larger than themselves. They have found a purpose and their mission in life.

This is one way you can orient yourself toward your greater purpose: **describe your life in one sentence**.

Clare Booth Luce was one of the first women to serve in Congress during the Kennedy administration. She was very worried that JFK couldn't get focused so that his legacy would be a mixed message of lots of little things. She said, "A great person is one sentence."

It can be difficult to reduce our purpose into one statement, but if we don't, we risk our life becoming a muddled paragraph. Those one or two sentences are your mission statement. Think about the mission statements of the following people:

Abraham Lincoln: "He fought to free slaves and bring equality to all people."

Walt Disney: "He wanted to make people happy."

Phil Knight, founder of Nike: "He brought inspiration and innovation to every athlete in the world."

Eric Schmidt, CEO of Google: "He is collecting all the world's information to make it accessible to everyone."

What would your one sentence look like? It's a big question. It takes most of us all our life to answer it.

MISSION CREEP

The secret of life is that there is no secret of life. It's all hard work.

People with goals succeed because they know where they're going. Mission creep happens when we lose focus and spend too much time on projects that don't get us any closer to our goals. We are attracted by all the choices that compete for our time and attention. Many people are plodding along at something but they aren't excelling because they're doing something they don't truly enjoy. It pays the bills, but doesn't fill them with a sense of purpose or achievement.

According to Mark Walton in his book, *Boundless Potential*, we are hardwired for reinvention and continuing success as we age. Walton asserts that by age fifty, we have undeveloped skills and intelligence that were not available to us during life's first half. As we get older, we face a choice: we can either retire our ambitions and downshift or we can choose to reinvent our course. Is it no wonder that we need to constantly re-evaluate our dreams, goals, and mission? Walton asserts that neuroscience confirms what the heart has already told us: we were created to continue growing and reinventing ourselves to suit our circumstances. The circumstances in which we find ourselves in middle age are not the same ones we faced in our college years, nor will they be the same as we approach retirement.

The late Stephen Covey reminded us that the place to start is the most inside part of ourselves because private victories always precede public victories. Our mission is a continuing process of renewal based on growth and maturity. Lasting happiness and fulfillment never comes from the outside in and are not achieved in one moment.

If we pursue the process of renewal through growth and maturity, our goals in life are bound to change as well. If we're not self-aware enough to recognize those changes, we end up letting others define who we are and what we want out of life.

"I find it fascinating that most people plan their vacation with better care than they do their lives. Perhaps that is because escape is easier than change."

—JIM ROHN

For many of us, our goals change over the years, but we're unaware of this internal shift because we don't look inward enough to even know it. It creeps up on us!

As with anything, we need to choose a direction.

"Would you tell me, please, which way I ought to go from here?""That depends a good deal on where you want to go," said the Cat. "I don't much care where—" said Alice. "Then it doesn't matter which way you go," said the Cat.

—LEWIS CARROLL

When your life gets chaotic, a mission statement is a map. When you are distracted, it's easy to slowly get off course. To prevent this, link your dreams and goals to your mission in life.

WHAT IS A MISSION STATEMENT?

If you don't know who you are, how can you know where you're going? These are the reasons I like a mission statement:

Summarizes purpose in life. In my own words, it connects my dreams and goals to my mission in life. A mission statement is not a list of goals. My goals are temporary and change with my circumstances; my mission statement provides me with a clear roadmap on how to achieve my goals.

Gives direction in life. Writing down my purpose and mission in life has forced me to think more seriously about the path I will need to take. A mission statement not only specifies what I intend to do, but also how I intend to not waste talents, skills, and strengths.

Defines success. It has helped me from settling for second best, or compromising, or giving up. It's been a document that has held me accountable to myself for the direction I'm headed in life. There are many things about my life I have not been able to choose or change. I cannot control everything in my life, but

I can choose how to respond to my circumstances in ways that dramatically increases my chance of success.

Clarifies role. I can assume any role in life that opportunity presents to me, but the title is not important. Roles may help me contribute toward my mission but they will come and go during my career. My mission continues with me throughout my life. *"Here is the test to find whether or not your mission on earth is finished: if you are alive, it isn't"*—Richard Bach

Reflects who I am. There are lots of other people who have plans for my life, if I let them. This is my chance to set my own priorities.

Provide a filter through which you can prioritize. I would recommend an ebook by Michael Hyatt called, *Michael Hyatt's Life Plan*. It makes a great point about the importance of saying yes to what matters most and saying no to those activities that matter less. A mission statement gives you clarity to manage your opportunities rather than be managed by them.

THE SEARCH FOR PURPOSE

Listen to that still, small voice within you.

The search for the purpose of life has been going on for thousands of years. Many spiritual leaders suggest that the search begins with God and not with the individual. In an effort to find an answer for myself, I completed the Ignatian Exercises a few years ago and found it to be a transformational experience that changed the way I search for meaning in my life.

The Ignatian Exercises are the product of the teachings of Ignatius of Loyola (1491-1556). Ignatius was a Spanish knight from a Basque noble family who founded the Society of Jesus, better known as the Jesuits. He originally formed a 30-day retreat of reflection for his monks where the participants were encouraged to enter into the silence of their heart and listen to the wisdom of their own experiences.

The retreat I attended followed the same guidelines outlined hundreds of years ago by Ignatius. One of our first assignments was to look for God's patterns in our life. Many of us could not pinpoint with clarity where God had ever shown up! Under the guidance of our retreat leaders, however, and with prayer and scripture readings, we were all led to see how God's hand had been on our shoulder, protecting and guiding, even in our most dire circumstances. It takes time to excavate the significance of our own stories.

> I found the Holy by going inward. I found my life's purpose by focusing first on myself, because the best way to understand the God who made me is to understand myself.

This is not the self-centered focus that we see in the media and in most self-help books. Personal connections start with the heart. I simply needed to understand God's language for me; once I did, I could then start to reach out and take hold of God in other ways. Finding the Holy somewhere "out there" was simply too ethereal because I found that I first needed to dig deeper inward.

Once I was able to listen to that still, small voice inside of me, I recognized it to be the still, small voice of God.

> *Then he was told, "Go, stand on the mountain at attention before God. God will pass by." A hurricane wind ripped through the mountain and shattered the rocks, but God wasn't to be found in the wind; after the wind an earthquake, but God wasn't in the earthquake; and after the earthquake a fire, but God wasn't in the fire; and after the fire, a gentle and quiet whisper.*
> *When Elijah heard the quiet voice, he muffled his face with his great cloak, went to the mouth of the cave, and stood there. A quiet voice asked, "So, Elijah, now tell me, what are you doing here?*
> —I KINGS 19:11-13 *THE MESSAGE*

We are asking the same questions: **Why am I here? What is my purpose**?

THINKING ABOUT MISSION

Points to Ponder: Never ask, Can I do this? Instead ask, how can I do this?

Inspiration: *"Let others lead small lives, but not you. Let others argue over small things, but not you. Let others cry over small hurts, but not you. Let others leave their future in someone else's hands, but not you."*—Jim Rohn

Reflection Question: What would my life look like if I were fully living out my mission?

PURPOSE TACTICS

DREAMS

Here is a two-step process that will help you uncover the answers to your dreams and purpose.

First Step: List the Things That Get Your Attention

Causes that I care about:

Things that upset me:

Things that make me happy, or sad:

Topics I always talk about with my friends:

Ideas that excite me:

Things that look, sound, and feel like an adventure:

Step Two: List Your Strengths

Things I am good at:

Things that make me feel good:

Talents I would be more excited to use:

My unique background or experience:

Now make a connection between those things that get your attention and your strengths. If you place them side-by-side, you can draw lines to make the connections. Or, you can prioritize and then number them.

You have interests and strengths that were given to you for a reason. How can you use them for good? When you find out, you'll be living your dream.

GOALS

Keep on track with your goals. Here are some suggestions:

Create an Inner Circle. We all have an inner circle of close friends, family, and others whom we interact with on a regular basis. To maximize their impact on your life, ask yourself whether they are the right people with whom you want closer interaction. By forging your inner circle with intention, you can collect people who reflect back your full potential.

Collect people who see the best in you and believe in your goals.

Eliminate people who take advantage of your generosity.

Protect yourself and fill your life with people whose values match your own.

Surround yourself with people who accept your gifts.

Find a Mentor. There are few people more valuable than mentors. They should be inspirational; more importantly, they need to be able to "see" you. They need to give you permission to keep charging ahead, keep chasing your goals, pushing past your failures, and keep making plans. Mentoring fills us with hope. Fill in the following sentences:

A great mentor in my life is   _____

I could be a mentor to   _____

I am inspired by   _____

Look for Adventure. Adventure is about taking risks, large and small, and this requires enthusiasm. It means stepping out into the unknown to discover your full potential. Staying open to new experiences is a daily adventure because you don't know what you'll find in those new experiences. Maybe you'll discover that you want to do something different, face or overcome a fear, write a new mission statement for yourself, or have a new vision for your life. Complacency and adventure cannot co-exist.

It would be fun to   _____

I would like to discover or learn   _____

It would be challenging to   _____

I would like to try   _____

I would step out of my comfort zone by   _____

MISSION

One of the quickest ways to gain clarity about whether
you are living your life in accordance to your mission
or purpose is to conduct a quick assessment. Assign a
numerical number between 1 and 10 to each area listed
below. 1 means "not at all satisfied" and 10 means "completely satisfied." Remember that a 10 doesn't necessarily
mean "perfect."

Area of Your Life	Your Rating (1-10)
Family	_____
Career	_____
Health	_____
Financial	_____
Education	_____
Recreation	_____
Charitable	_____
Spiritual	_____
Adventure	_____
Travel	_____
Romance	_____
Relationships	_____

Note that 6's and 7's are the most difficult numbers
because they mean you're not unhappy enough to do

anything about it, but a long way from being satisfied, too. In other words, "you've settled."

Delete every number that is not an 8, 9 or 10. Either you have what you want or you don't. Anything below an 8 means you are not fully living out your mission or purpose. You don't have what you want but you haven't faced up to it yet.

Everyone is on the same journey, but some of us have better road maps. Dreams, goals, and a mission provide us with a way to embark on the journey we want to be on, and not someone else's plan for our life. Our mind is our strongest currency. To follow our purpose in life, we will need courage.

CHAPTER 3

COURAGE

"It is God who arms me with strength and makes my way perfect. God makes my feet like the feet of a deer; God enables me to stand on the heights. God trains my hands for battle; my arms can bend a bow of bronze. You give me your shield of victory, and your right hand sustains me; you stoop down to make me great. You broaden the path beneath me, so that ankles do not turn."

—PSALM 18:32-36

Most people do not react with enthusiasm when the FBI comes knocking at their door. It usually means either they, or someone they know, is in trouble.

My surveillance team had identified a person who was in contact with Igor, a suspected intelligence officer. I ran a background check on the individual, a man named Elmo Hattan who lived in a run-down part of the city. When I knocked on the door, a large, overweight man who had not shaved for several days opened it. He smiled initially, until he saw my FBI credentials, and the gap-toothed smiled turned into a scowl. "What do you want?" he demanded.

I introduced my colleague and asked if we could come in and ask him a couple of questions about his association with Igor. He looked at our credentials, grunted, and motioned with his head for us to come inside. Elmo wore an unbuttoned denim shirt with a dingy white, stained T-shirt underneath. His hair was rumpled and he wore no shoes. I'm not prissy, and have stepped in enough cow dung in my day to not flinch at many smells or stains, but as I looked at his discolored couch and torn chair, I opted to stand for the interview. So did Elmo.

There was no way to ease into the conversation without telling Elmo straight up that he had been observed in the company of Igor, a person of interest to an FBI investigation. Elmo glared at both of us while I explained that we were hoping he could shed some light on Igor's activities.

Elmo did not smile. He did not say a word.

I continued by emphasizing we weren't investigating Elmo and that our interests centered on Igor. Elmo replied in a harsh voice, "You've been following me."

"No," I assured him. "It was Igor we were following." I hastened to add that we didn't suspect Igor of being involved in any criminal activity.

At that point, Elmo came toward me, like a bull about ready to charge. I didn't move—I had faced something bigger than Elmo in my past...

I grew up miles from the nearest small town. It was a rough childhood. The biggest danger to my life was rattlesnakes—not drugs. I spent my summers fixing fence and shoveling out irrigation ditches. My grandmother had "ammo" on her Christmas list!

The ranch covered several thousands of acres and we ran hundreds of head of cattle. When I was 10 years old, I was riding my black quarter horse and helping Dad corral bulls. He was further up the creek but he told me to round up an old horned bull that he wanted to sell.

Unfortunately for me, the bull was with a bunch of cows and did not want to leave. Yet my horse was a good cutting horse, and cut the bull off as he tried to dodge past us.

Then the bull turned, horns first, and charged my horse. The horse reared and I grabbed the saddle horn. I felt the weight shift under me as the bull's head hit my horse's shoulder. I knew that wherever that horse was going, I was going too.

This was not the time to get bucked off, but I knew deep down in my boots I wouldn't be, I'd ride that horse no matter what he did. My horse pivoted on his hind feet in the opposite direction and we got away.

For a ten-year-old, I was in what you might call an "emergency situation."

If I returned to the corral without that bull, I might have been better off to deal with the horns than my Dad's temper. He had no tolerance for excuses or failure.

My horse was spooked. He was trembling, breathing hard, and flaring his nostrils as he exhaled. I was shaking, too, and I know that he sensed my fear was as great as his.

I was scared, and knew there was no rescue.

I told myself:

Don't run

Don't panic

Face the situation

Evaluate your environment

Believe you can do it

Fix it as soon as possible

Waiting to act will only make the situation worse

Now is the best time

I am the best person

It took a few minutes, but my horse finally settled down. The bull remained alert and watched both of us from a distance of a few yards. I knew I had to go right back and find a way to get that bull to the corral. I was afraid that next time the bull charged, his horns might gore my horse and I'd be left with no way to escape. My heart was racing and my palms were sweaty, but I would not be defeated.

I knew the sight of my horse agitated the bull so I took a chance and got off, hoping the bull would calm down. I wiped the sweat from the palms of my hands on my pants and stood still for a moment. The bull looked at me, then shook his head so hard I could see streams of snot fling toward me, but he didn't move forward. I softly said something like, "shoo" and gently waved my arms. Another angry toss of the head, but after a minute, he slowly turned and moved in the direction of the corral with the little herd of cows. One by one, the cows lost interest in being trailed toward the corral and dropped off until it was just the bull and one cow. I stayed back far enough that the bull didn't feel rushed and I led my horse behind me. As we neared the corral, I got back on my horse so my Dad would think I'd cut the bull off with my expert horsemanship. When he saw the bull and me coming, he waved to me to signal "Good job."

Now, what happened between Dad and that bull when they got face to face is another story for another time ... but in my part of it, I learned several lessons about how to be strong minded and keep moving ahead when faced with the unknown.

As Elmo barged toward me, he stopped within inches of my face. I didn't flinch. He had not succeeded in intimidating me. My colleague had moved nearer to me and was prepared to pull Elmo away and arrest him for assaulting a federal officer if he touched me. I smiled, handed Elmo my business card, and left. Igor was recalled to Moscow shortly afterward—no explanation was given, but the FBI suspected the Russian government was concerned that Igor's questionable contacts and activities could become an embarrassment.

I'm not the only child or adult who has experienced a racing heart and sweaty palms—perhaps there's an important meeting in the morning and you are asking questions: Am I ready? What if I mess up? Time is short and you feel anxious. Researchers[6] have determined that a little anxiety may be just what you need to focus your attention and energy so you can perform at your peak. Somewhere between freaked out and checked out is the anxiety sweet spot: motivated enough to succeed and yet not so anxious that you falter.

If you're not pushing the boundaries enough to produce a healthy dose of anxiety, you're not at peak performance. If you do not feel scared, there is no reason for you to be courageous.

BE COURAGEOUS

You can look at hostile situations in a positive and proactive way.

Objectively survey your situation. I thought about my situation before getting down from my horse. At ten, I was not tall enough to get back into the saddle because the stirrups were too far off the ground. So I never dismounted unless I knew I could find a way to get back on—I saw a rock-pile nearby and quickly determined that if the bull kept charging, I could scramble to safety on the rock-pile.

Look at your situation accurately and make a decision even if you don't have all the data. The probability that you will be able to collect enough information to be 100% certain of the outcome is very minimal, particularly in fast-moving situations. Make small assessments continually so you can respond quickly and effectively as your environment or circumstance continues to change and shift.

Keep the larger goal in focus. My goal was to get the bull to the corral. Everything I did enabled me to move closer to my goal. I could have gotten sidetracked with worrying about several other things as I stepped down from my horse. I was not irresponsible, but I took calculated risks. My alternative was to do nothing and be satisfied with—what? I would have accepted defeat in the face of a challenge, reinforcing a negative pattern of behavior of surrender and compliance that would have would have stayed with me the rest of my life.

Always be ready to take the initiative. Don't wait for a new career, or relationship, or other opportunities to come to you. Go and actively meet your challenge. If you want something, go for it. No one else is going to live your life for you—this is the one thing for which you are totally responsible. You can change your circumstances if you keep the larger goal in focus and never let it slip out of sight.

Balance hope and fear. I didn't know how much courage I had until I looked fear in the eye, stepped off my horse, and moved in front of the bull. The pain I experienced in facing my fear was far less than if I'd run away from the opportunity to develop my courage.

In the long run, taking action is less painful than wallowing in fear. Building your courage is a smarter choice than running from your fears. Opportunity is veiled by fear. Your greatest regrets in life will not be the mistakes you made; they will be the opportunities you missed.

Expose yourself to danger. To engage and defeat a superior foe, sometimes you will need to embrace danger. All opportunities bring danger with them because they bring risk and danger of the unknown. Leaders see those opportunities and do the right thing in spite of the danger.

The situations that demand your courage are blessings to you because they expose your fears. When you are scared, you are facing your fears. Remember this: whatever you fear, you must eventually face. The fear you feel does not need to weigh you down; instead, it can deepen your resolve. A strong mind is not built on something that is slapped together on a shallow foundation. It needs solid rock—like a skyscraper, the higher you want to go, the deeper you must go.

THE NATURE OF COURAGE

Boldness comes from your head; courage comes from your heart.

Boldness is a cerebral activity that recognizes opportunities, creates plans, and assesses the danger. Courage is a visceral reaction that comes from your gut. Courage does not require a life or death situation to make itself known. You face situations every day where courage is required. It is needed whenever you venture out of your comfort zone and take on something that challenges the status quo.

The need for courage usually manifests itself in fight-or-flight moments. At some point you face the fear—speaking in public, leaving an unfulfilling relationship, starting a new career—and choose to do what is right in spite of the personal risks you face. Courage is the ability to take a chance without knowing the result.

If you refuse to face your fear, it's almost impossible to grow because, in its simplest form, all behavior is the product of either fear or desire. Fear is not something to be avoided. A strong mind recognizes fear for what it is—a sign that you need to face the issue or obstacle in front of you.

Let's explore the fundamental aspects of courage: heart, adventure, and trust.

THINKING ABOUT COURAGE

Points to Ponder: To live the life of faith, you must first stop making excuses for your fears.

Inspiration: *"If you're not living on the edge, you're taking up too much space."*—Will Willis

Reflection Question: What does overcoming a fear of your fears look like?

HEART

"Few are those who see with their own eyes and feel with their own hearts."

—ALBERT EINSTEIN

When I was six years old, my grandfather bought my brother and me a black and white Shetland pony that we named Socks. I was thrilled because I now had a horse of my very own and one small enough I could reach the stirrups to get on. Grandfather also bought us a new black saddle with silver trim and a matching bridle. I was overjoyed with our new present.

I quickly learned that Shetland ponies are strong-willed creatures who are not above using their superior strength to make life miserable for their six-year-old riders. Unfortunately for me at this time in my young life, Dad was an excellent horseman and I wanted to be just like him. He would say, "If you can't learn to ride that pony, you'll never get a bigger horse."

A love/hate relationship grew between Socks and me. He would reach around and bite my toe as soon as I saddled up and got on. When I tried to ride him around the yard, he'd stubbornly refuse to move beyond the barn. I'd kick him hard on the ribs but he'd only balk worse. I was scared of Socks because I was afraid he'd buck me off if I became more aggressive. I tried leading him out of the yard and down onto the East Meadow before I got on, but as soon as I got back on, he ran back to the barn. Worse yet, when Dad got on him, he behaved beautifully. My humiliation was complete because Dad saw that I couldn't control the pony.

110

I wouldn't be the one in control until I had the courage to face my fear of being bucked off. One day I managed to get Socks out of the yard and was riding him east of the ranch house when we came across a ditch to cross. I grabbed the saddle horn and urged him on. As he jumped, he bucked. My hand slid off the horn so I held on with my knees pressed into his ribs. He bucked again, and I slid further to the left, grasping at empty air as I tried to find the saddle horn. I also lost control of the reins. The third buck sent me flying through the air. I saw a barbed wire fence in front of me and grabbed for the top wire as I landed. I caught part of it with one hand as I covered my face with the other. I didn't have on gloves and felt the barbed wire cut through the palm of my hand. My heavy jeans and boots kept the rest of me from getting sliced up.

Socks turned and ran back to the barn as fast as his stubby little legs could take him. I had to walk home, but that day I realized there was no more fear of the unknown when it came to being bucked off. I had moved into it and survived. Socks sensed a change in my attitude as well, because he became more cooperative and we got along better. I never liked Socks, though, so my Grandfather rewarded me with a quarter horse big enough that I had to find rocks to use as a stepladder for several years to come.

This must have been about the time I came to idolize John Wayne—not just because of his Western movies but because he was quoted as saying, *"Courage is being scared to death, but saddling up anyway."* I knew just what he meant because it took all the courage I had to saddle Socks and wait to be humiliated—yet again.

I've always liked John Wayne's definition of courage because it implies that courage is the ability to pick yourself up and move into action in spite of fear. Courageous people are still afraid, but they don't let fear paralyze them. Once you give in to fear, a pattern begins to develop. Each time you avoid a fear, and feel relieved that you have avoided it, the behavior is reinforced so that in the future you continue to avoid the fear by giving in to it. It becomes a vicious cycle.

If you listen carefully, however, there is a tiny voice inside that is saying: you will die full of regrets for a life that might have been if you do not move beyond your fears. At your deepest level, you were created to move forward with your heart. The word "courage" is derived from the Latin word "cor," which means heart.

At the core of courage is your heart.

Your heart expresses the person you are truly meant to be. Only through courage can you be empowered to move into the unknown without fear.

There is a strong connection between a strong mind and the heart. If your path has a heart, you know deep down that it is the right one for you. If you have taken a path without a heart and one that does not have a deep connection to your heart, that path has the potential to destroy you.

THE PATH WITH NO HEART

It doesn't take courage to follow the easy path.

There's a long check-off list before agents are assigned to undercover operations. A standard psychological evaluation from the FBI's Behavioral Science Unit sifts out the James Bond wannabes who confuse real life with snippets of movie fantasy. After they are identified and eliminated, the rest of us move on to the larger problem of how to approach our targets in a way that won't arouse their suspicion. Undercover work will always be more of an art than a science because there are no hard and fast rules on what works and what doesn't. A rigorous routine of surveillance and interviews will usually reveal the soft underbelly of any target, but the undercover agent must be able to carry it off—yes, *really* well. The subtle guerilla warfare techniques employed by the FBI spawn a special brand of paranoia among criminals and foreign agents who find themselves in the FBI's crosshairs.

When I met a fellow agent named Leo, I was impressed. He was a tall, good-looking guy with loads of wavy dark hair that fell over the collar of his starched white shirt. He was affable, extroverted, and always made a good impression. He seemed competent and capable, and I thought he would end up as Special Agent in Charge of an FBI field office someday.

Top FBI management refer to themselves as the Front Office, and they needed someone who had been vetted by the Behavioral Science Unit to work as a UCA against a violent motorcycle gang in the area. It was a high-level case with lots of interest by FBI Headquarters and other law enforcement agencies. The budget was huge; the UCA could drive a Mercedes if he wanted—the sky was the limit.

Leo had no experience in working gangs and was unfamiliar with those types of cases. The Front Office thought this would work in their favor. He would be a totally fresh face against the criminals they were trying to indict, so they approached Leo. No one is sure why, but he said yes.

I didn't know Leo well, but those who did were worried about him from the very beginning. Leo had always seemed more comfortable working white-collar fraud cases. Leo wore suits, white shirts, and a tie to work everyday. No one thought he was UCA material against a motorcycle gang. It was a plum assignment, though, and if he were successful, he'd become a legend in the Bureau. Movie scripts have been written about undercover agents who bring in bad guys in this league—the case was that big.

Typical of deep undercover cases where the UCA's life could be endangered if compromised by FBI contact, the only ones who met with Leo were his supervisor and case agent. Finally, after a two-year investigation, the word came down that the takedown would be imminent and several members of the gang would be indicted.

I was part of the raid. We met at an auditorium at five o'clock in the morning with around one hundred federal, state, and local law enforcement officers all decked out in bulletproof vests, shotguns, and semi-automatics. It looked like a high school assembly with everyone talking and moving around.

The supervisor stood on the stage and gave everyone their assignment and broke us down into ten teams. There were ten houses to be searched and fifteen suspects to be arrested. All of them were considered armed and dangerous. For this reason, FBI SWAT would be leading the arrest teams into each house. Many of the folks we were looking to arrest were just getting home from a night out.

My team set up around the perimeter of one of the houses and waited while a member of the FBI SWAT knocked and announced, "FBI." No answer, so another knock and announce. Enough time had passed so the battering ram was brought up and the door was smashed off its hinges. Within seconds, all the suspects inside the house were in handcuffs and brought out by the SWAT agents.

One of them was Leo.

I couldn't believe what I was seeing. Leo's once beautiful dark wavy hair was now gray and tangled. He had gained about thirty pounds and had a beard. I knew it was Leo, though, by his eyes, always a brilliant light blue.

Leo was arrested in his undercover name so that suspicion would not fall upon him as being a federal agent. If he were not arrested with the others, it would look as though Leo had become an informant. The FBI had enough evidence so that Leo never had to testify in court and reveal his true identity.

Leo was brought back into the office as a case agent. I heard he was having trouble on many levels. He had started drinking, showing up drunk for work at nine o' clock in the morning, his marriage was on the rocks, and he had isolated himself from his FBI colleagues. He had become "unmanageable," to use the phrase put out by the Front Office, and was assigned to my squad where management felt they could keep a closer eye on him.

Leo had taken a path with no heart when he took the undercover assignment. The opportunity for publicity and promotion was a temptation that he could not let pass. The Front Office would not have forced him to take the UCA position. In fact, they go to extra efforts to make sure there is good match between personality and the assignment. The choice was Leo's and he made a bad one.

> It's important to remember that courageous people are still afraid, but they don't let fear paralyze them. If they make a mistake, they admit it so they can move on.

Leo could not admit he made a mistake. He could have been replaced by another UCA, but his fear of failure was greater than his need to be courageous.

When he came out of undercover work, he talked to authors and publishers about telling his story but they soon lost interest when they realized he had drinking problems. If Leo had been expecting a movie deal about his life, it didn't happen. While he had done a great job as a UCA, FBI Headquarters didn't bring him back to teach new agents or undercover classes at Quantico—again, because of his drinking problem.

Leo was never promoted and his reputation continued to spiral downwards. He retired early from the FBI. He and his wife divorced and he still chooses to distance himself from his FBI colleagues.

The path with no heart is strewn with broken bodies.

THE PATH WITH HEART

The path with heart is motivated by the right reasons.

> *"Remembering that I'll be dead soon is the most important tool I've ever encountered to help me make the big choices in life. Because almost everything—all external expectations, all pride, all fear of embarrassment or failure—these things just fall away in the face of death, leaving only what is truly important. Remembering that you are going to die is the best way I know to avoid the trap of thinking you have something to lose. You are already naked. There is no reason not to follow your heart."*
>
> —STEVE JOBS

Leo's sad story is like many others who do not have the courage to look at their lives and choose to take a different path, one that has more meaning for them. Newspapers, magazines, and tabloids are full of stories about people who believed that money, fame, or power would bring them fulfillment. They are motivated by the wrong values. Based on reports of drug abuse, divorce, and increased violence, I'll let you be the judge of how well that strategy works for them.

Based on outward appearances, Leo was a man of courage. How could a fearful man live and work among a gang of violent criminals for two years? Yet, there was a deep fear inside Leo that kept prodding him forward, even as it was wrecking his health and personal life. Many of the agents talked about Leo's situation over coffee, and the general consensus was pride and ego kept him tethered to the undercover operation.

However, when I consulted the Behavioral Science Unit on several of my cases, I was encouraged to get beneath the ego and image we all present to the world to uncover the basic fears and desires that motivate behavior. Leo was no different than George or Nicholas—until they were able to get in touch with their true nature, they were unable to identify either their fears or desires.

Steve Jobs is one of countless others who has inspired us with his courage to look into his deepest part to find that spark of life that will bring real meaning to life. Heart is not about money, fame, or power.

Heart is always the spirit of courage.

Everyone wants to be courageous. We love our heroes! From the Bible to fairy tales to Hollywood movies, we are drawn to tales of bravery and self-sacrifice. Courage inspires us. It is something everyone wants—but it is impossible to find without heart.

The path to my heart has always touched upon my deepest fears. Fear is usually the one thing that gets in the way of pursuing the path with heart. As an adult who genuinely desires to fully be the person God created me to be, I recognized I needed courage to move beyond my fears.

THINKING ABOUT HEART

Points to Ponder: Chose a path that has your heart as well as your head.

Inspiration: *"Beware what you set your heart upon, for it surely shall be yours."*—Ralph Waldo Emerson.

Reflection Question: When have you needed courage to follow your heart?

ADVENTURE

"Death is more universal than life; everyone dies but not everyone lives."

—ALAN SACHS

Our ranch house was surrounded by rugged mountains and every day after school my brother and I would gather up our stick guns and grandmother's rusty old traps to set off to explore the world around us.

In my mind, I was Daniel Boone on a daring adventure because the ranch house was surrounded by all sorts of interesting things like rocks, rattle snakes, mountains, rivers, and wildlife—for a kid with an imagination, it was Candyland on steroids!

After school, we played with abandon all year long as we let the sun heat up our backs and the cold winters nip at our heels. When I recall my childhood stories, I tell people about riding over a rattle snake on my bicycle, getting bucked off my horse and landing in a barbed wire fence, getting lost in the mountains trying to find a great-uncle's moonshine still, and watching a mountain lion attack an old horse on the east meadow.

Perhaps these things were not safe by today's standards, but for me they held the pulse of life. My childhood was not boring. This was one of the greatest gifts God could have given me—an appreciation for adventure. I still hear the call to adventure through an inner voice, beckoning me to something that moves me beyond the ordinary—and yes, beyond what is safe, sometimes.

The call to adventure will be different for everyone, but that is what makes us wonderful and unique. Life is an amazing journey—and you alone are responsible for the quality of it. It is not an obligation; it is an adventure.

BE ADVENTUREOUS

Here are three practices that can empower you to overcome obstacles that are preventing you from living a life of adventure:

1. Examine the labels you give yourself. The labels that others gave me didn't matter as much as the ones I gave myself. Those that were self-imposed became boundaries that limited how I could move forward. Subconsciously, I wouldn't let myself cross them.

2. Empower from the inside. Empowerment is an attitude that is quiet and tranquil; it's not noisy and fragmented. Empowerment comes by having a steady purpose—a goal. To attain my goal, I needed to believe I could accomplish it. Then my goals and purpose came into sharper focus.

3. Let Go of Ego. Ego was the most difficult obstacle to overcome. Approaching life with a sense of adventure meant embracing the unknown and learning new things—from everything about myself to my new situation. Ego can be a tremendous impediment to achieving the truly difficult things in my life because I don't want to admit I don't know everything. Here are some ways I let go of ego:

Resist the temptation to complain—ego strengthens itself by complaining. In what areas are you complaining? This could be where the adventure is waiting.

Avoid negative reactions—grievances and resentments are a way to punish others. In what areas do you have resentment? This could be where the adventure is waiting.

Forget about being right— the ego loves to be right. In what areas do you feel the need to be right? This could be where the adventure is waiting.

INTO THE UNKNOWN

No pain, no gain.

While at the FBI Academy's four-month training program, instructors for new agents made certain we were out of our comfort zone every day. No matter how experienced we happened to be in one area of discipline, we were either pushed further in that area, or toward an area where we were not as experienced.

A typical day at the Academy ran like this: mornings might begin with interview and interrogation techniques. We took turns interviewing people suspected of various federal crimes. Assistant U.S. attorneys came into our classrooms and prepped us with real cases. Actors would assume the role of the individuals involved in the crime and new agents would interview them.

Reading body language and deciphering verbal communication became critical in uncovering the truth. The interviews were videotaped and then critiqued in front of your new agent's class. Every mistake and misspoken word was painfully highlighted for all to see.

The rest of the day might become more physical. Many of our tactical exercises were stress courses on the firearms range that tested our psychological reactions to hostile situations, physical ability to continue to move forward, and listening to our gut instinct when making split-second decisions.

Once our physical fitness instructors found our areas of weakness, their dry little hearts made it their mission to push us as far into that discomfort zone as possible. Many of the obstacles were as much psychological as physical. Since I had trouble with push-ups, my coach made sure he was the one to count each and every push-up for our interim Fitness Indicator Test (FIT). He'd start out counting every push-up, "One, two, three, four," and so on. And then we'd hit a magic number and he'd keep counting, "Nine, nine, nine, nine." I did the ninth pushup nine times before he finally counted it! All the while I'm thinking, "I don't have any physical reserves left." "I've wasted them on the ninth push-up." "Can I make it?" I finished that particular test missing the critical points needed to graduate from the Academy.

Before I had time to plan how to make up the points at the next FIT, I got to start again—this time in firearms where life-size cutouts of mobsters, bank robbers, and terrorists were sprinkled through the mock city at the FBI Academy called "Hogan's Ally." These figures popped up in front of you, sometimes with a baby as a hostage, sometimes with a gun, and sometimes with a white flag of surrender. It's called a stress test because it's timed and you are required to make split second decisions on whether to shoot the pop-up figure, try to save the kidnapped victim, or move on to the next target.

One of our instructors would shout, "Are you feeling the pain yet?" "Is this still easy?" After I had convinced myself that I hadn't joined a bunch of sadists, I began to appreciate how my relationship with anxiety was changing. To survive in this environment, I had to begin to look at discomfort as my ally. My feelings of discomfort were a signal that I was venturing out of the familiar zone. If I wanted to stay comfortable, I should have stayed at my old job and my old way of thinking.

A life of adventure has no rigid formulas. What if the mother of Moses in the Old Testament of the Bible had warned Moses against playing with fire and he spent the rest of his life carefully avoiding all burning bushes? Things happen and if we're wise, we'll listen to that inner voice that is pointing us to something bigger, better, and bolder.

Your decisions do not always have to be right, but there is something very powerful about having the courage to take action.

Never ask, can I do this? Instead ask, how can I do this?

To live a life of adventure takes courage because you will be moving from the safety and predictability of the known into the volatile and changeable landscape of the unknown. It is the responsibility of the explorer to find a way.

THINKING ABOUT ADVENTURE

Points to Ponder: Most people don't aim too high and miss. They aim too low and hit.

Inspiration: *"Life is either a daring adventure or nothing at all."*—Helen Keller

Reflection Question: When is the last time you did something you've never done before—something that made you feel a bit uncomfortable?

TRUST

"We are never so vulnerable than when we trust someone, but paradoxically, if we cannot trust, neither can we find love or joy."

—WALTER ANDERSON

People ask me how I could create trust when I lied to the targets of my undercover investigation about my identity. I never looked at it as though I was lying to them about the important things in life. As I discussed in the first chapter on authenticity, I only ran into trouble in undercover cases when I tried to be someone other than who I really am, beneath the surface.

Most of my career was spent as a case agent and not an undercover agent. Building trust is also difficult when developing human intelligence sources (HUMINT)— people from the community who knew and worked with the spy I was trying to recruit. These are people I met in my true name and identity. I still could not always be as transparent as they (or I) would have liked in discussing my future plans because that information was classified.

I found these interactions to be a straddle between interrogation and conversation, never daring to cross over too far in either direction. I needed their cooperation so I tried to keep the interaction all very conversational, and yet they were meeting and doing business with a member of a hostile intelligence service. The security of the United States was at stake, so there were times when I felt the need to dig my teeth in and—yes, interrogate.

Trust ran both ways. I trusted them not to run back to the spy and divulge every detail of my conversation with them. How can we build the trust needed for authentic conversation in an era of deceit and cynicism? It is tempting to be judgmental about what is, or is not, considered to be a lie. Here are a couple of considerations to keep in mind.

First, remember that people deceive themselves as much as they deceive others. People are capable of deceiving themselves into believing any number of things—sometimes they exaggerate their own importance or abilities to impress others. Sometimes they're too critical of their own efforts and don't give themselves enough credit for their accomplishments. We know what it feels like to fall into the snare of self-deception or self-limiting beliefs—with luck, only briefly. The incredible thing about self-deception is that not only are we telling a lie, but it's ourselves we are lying to! We all have blind spots about our own performance and the better we're able to understand them, the more empowered we will be.

Secondly, not all deceit is equal. All of us have taken steps to improve ourselves in the sight of others. This is cosmetic deceit and it refers to our efforts to make ourselves look better than we are. It can be a dab of make-up to hide a blemish or the use of words to hide an imperfection in our work performance that we'd rather not broadcast to the world. I've used cosmetic deceit when dealing with others as well, such as compliments on hair, performance, or a sermon with the intention of making the other person feel better and soften the edges of an embarrassment.

I used deceit on a superficial level when
working undercover counterintelligence cases.

When the need came to develop authentic trust, however, the
undercover agent was "cutout" and replaced by an FBI agent uti-
lizing their true identity. Authentic trust is impossible to build if
it is based on deception or ulterior motives. You can only move
to a certain point in a relationship if it is not built around trust,
so the undercover agents were moved out to bring in agents who
could move the relationship to the next step.

Authentic trust is built when there's a commitment to the
relationship. In the same way, authentic conversations are built
when there's a commitment to growing and deepening the relationship, not just to maintain the status quo. If the relationship is
the central consideration, mutual commitments are essential to
avoid concerns about manipulation or control in the conversation. A strong mind is one that is courageous in building/creat-
ing relationships with authentic trust.

A few years ago, Joel and Ethan Coen produced a movie
called *Fargo*. It was set in rural Minnesota in the dead of winter
and tells the story of a kidnapping case that goes deadly wrong.
Those of us who saw the movie will never forget the sight of a
pregnant Marge Gunderson trudging through cold and snow to
investigate the crime.

The opening credits announced that the movie is based on a
true story. Journalists could not find any reference to the crime de-
picted in the movie, and eventually the producers admitted that
it was all fiction. The Coen brothers explained that they believed

that if the movie were represented as a true story, it would have more credibility with the audience.

We enter into relationships with the same desire for honesty because experience has shown that honesty is the foundation upon which trust is built. People assess information differently when they believe it's true.

TRUSTING OTHERS MAKES YOU FEEL GOOD

Why do people cooperate with each other when it's not always in their best interests to do so?

Why do people choose trust over skepticism and generosity over selfishness? In a recent study, researchers[7] from Emory University in Atlanta made an interesting discovery: People co-operate with others because it makes them feel good. They act this way because the brain is hard-wired to cooperate—it associates cooperation with reward. We've long associated cooperation with creativity and greater productivity, but this study provides a new way to explore our innate desire to trust and cooperate with others.

The Bible reminds us in the book of Ephesians that when we do good unto others, we are most fully ourselves. We are empowered when we have the courage to trust others:

When you look for the good in others, they will show it to you. When you appreciate the worth in others, it's easy for them to be their best.

When you accept others, they show you their strengths.

When you notice others, they feel like they belong and are special.

When you need others, they feel the good in themselves.

When you look for the beauty in others, you will discover your own best self.

When you bring out the best in others, you make powerful friends.

When you find the gift of others, you find reasons to believe in yourself.

THINKING ABOUT TRUST

Points to Ponder: Learn to trust the wisdom of your heart.

Inspiration: *"To be trusted is a greater compliment than being loved."*—George MacDonald

Reflection Question: How do you know when you can trust someone?

COURAGE TACTICS

HEART

People who take a path with heart will need courage to face their fears. It's important to develop a deeper awareness of our fears and understand how they are preventing us from moving forward in certain areas of our life. Here are some suggestions for you:

Identify your 5 biggest fears. Listen to what your inner voice is telling you about how each one of these fears is affecting different areas of your life.

_____

_____

_____

_____

_____

Think of a situation as an adult when you felt afraid, yet chose to face your fear. What did you observe, think, and feel at the time? What did you do to help you face your fear? At what point did your fear start to go down?

Think of a situation you are currently facing that creates fear or anxiety. What are you most afraid of?

Get in touch with your gut—what is your first reaction when you think of how your fear is impacting: career, relationships, spiritual growth, travel, family, finances, health, and education. If you had the courage, would you be doing something different?

Write down 5 activities that would help you overcome each fear.

_____

_____

_____

_____

_____

Rank the activities from high to low in terms of producing anxiety. Start with the activity that would be the most effective in achieving your goal and work your way down the list.

If you feel that any step is too big, then break it down into smaller steps.

ADVENTURE

These are the steps you can take to develop the courage to move into a bigger adventure for your life:

1. Ask tough questions. What is the cost of your continued inaction? Will you feel regret at the end of your life for what you didn't do? Do the benefits outweigh the costs? What are the consequences if you don't move out of your rut?

2. Notice your fear. It is normal to experience fear or anxiety. It is vitally important, however, that you are not controlled by it. Feelings of fear can be nothing more than an indication you are on the right path. Continue to notice the fear or anxiety but keep pushing through it. Often, this is the difference between those who succeed and those who fail.

3. Listen to your intuition. There are certain situations that are well and truly dangerous; listen to your gut instinct. If you are in danger of physical or emotional harm, do not move forward. Instead, you may need to jump a barrier and *move outward* in order to find a place of safety.

4. Accept accountability. It is easy to become entrenched in old patterns of thinking which can cloud your judgment. If a friend were considering the same action you are contemplating, would you encourage them to do it? Take a step back and ask friends that you trust to help you achieve your goals or their opinion on the action you are contemplating. These friends need to be ones you can trust who have your best interests at heart.

5. Create memorial stones. Take a moment to memorialize your achievements. Choosing to move into a discomfort zone takes courage and it's important to celebrate this important achievement by marking the moment. You may want to journal your experience. Memorialize the things you did to work your way through a discomfort zone.

6. Take time to reflect. You are creating new thinking patterns that, in turn, will continue to influence future situations. Reflect on the ways in which you are no longer stuck in a behavior that creates fear and anxiety. What did you do well? What would you do differently next time? How will this help you move into your next discomfort zone?

TRUST

It takes courage to reach out and trust people, and have them trust you. Here are some ways you can develop trust with others.

Share some personal and accurate information about yourself. How can you expect others to trust you if you don't trust them with personal information in return?

Be trustworthy in small things. If you can't be trusted to follow through on small things, why should others trust you with something more important?

Do not gossip. Keeping your word and the confidences of others builds trust and signals that you're in the relationship to stay.

Do not omit important details. It is living the details of life, when you think no one is looking, that you are most your true self. People around you do notice how you live your life, and they make decisions—subconsciously, often—about your trustworthiness. If you neglect to share the important and telling details of your life, you risk being perceived as deceitful.

Be transparent. If you are open and honest about your goals and dreams in life, you will establish firm ground upon which to build your relationship.

Building trusting relationships is a personal choice anyone can make. The type of communication that builds trust between people involves observing your own behavior as much as observing the behavior of the other person.

A strong mind has the courage to embrace their fear and move out of their comfort zone so they can take the path that leads to their heart. It has the courage to move forward when faced with challenges and adversity. This is difficult to do if you do not have confidence.

CHAPTER 4

CONFIDENCE

"Believe in yourself! Have faith in your abilities!
Without a humble but reasonable confidence
in your own powers you cannot be successful
or happy."

—NORMAN VINCENT PEALE

I was sworn in as an FBI agent at the J. Edgar Hoover building in Washington D.C. on a Monday morning in 1983. All I remember of that whirlwind event was meeting the FBI Director, William Webster, in a conference room with the forty-one other new agents in my class. We stood in a circle and were sworn in as new agents-in-training as a group; however, we would not get our credentials and hand weapons until we completed a four month training program at the FBI Academy. We sat in alphabetical order that morning—my last name was Stumbough—and continued in the same seating pattern the next four months.

By early afternoon that same day, a bus took us all to the Academy on the Marine Corp base at Quantico, Virginia. Eight women and thirty-four men checked into dormitory rooms with thin carpets, small windows, and no televisions. Each new agent's class was assigned to the same floor to build camaraderie—women and men in different rooms.

We were given no time to look over our new surroundings. Instead, we were told to change into our gym clothes to begin our training program that afternoon. A high degree of importance is placed on physical fitness at the Academy so our counselors were anxious to put us in competition with each other in push-ups, pull-ups, and a two-mile run as soon as we arrived.

As agents-in-training, we were competing for points in the physical fitness (FIT) test, for failure to accumulate enough FIT scores could result in dismissal from the Academy. The competition to be selected as an FBI agent is intense since there are thousands of applicants for every one position available. It's not an exaggeration to say that our entire new agents' class was a competitive group of people. We all felt pressure not only to perform for the points, but also to impress each other.

I was nervous. While I had scored very high in the scholastic and personality tests, I was not an athlete. Riding horses and working cattle had not prepared me for the intensity with which my colleagues and instructors approached the Bureau's rigorous physical requirements.

When I took the FIT that afternoon, I was the 1% that makes the top 99% possible.

I failed miserably. My challenge then became twofold: maintaining confidence in myself while training to pass the rigid test.

If I am to be honest, there was a point when I began to wonder whether I had made the wrong choice in pursuing the FBI. Was I too bullheaded to read the writing on the wall? Should I give up? While these questions were whirling around my head, the one that held the most power was this one: Is the FBI still my goal or not? If not, I should leave the Academy and focus on a goal that inspired me.

This was a healing process for me because it took me back to the roots of my decision to become an FBI Agent. As I traced the choices, conversations, and events that led to the letter from FBI Headquarters recommending me for a special agent position. I realized that, to achieve something bigger and bolder, I needed to become bigger and bolder myself. I kept my eye on my goal. God's hand was upon my shoulders and I knew this career would change me as a person—into the person I was created to be.

I could complain all I wanted, but the truth of the matter is that I had not taken the time needed to build up my upper body strength. I had no physical limitations other than those imposed by my mind.

BE CONFIDENT

I worked with a coach at the Academy who taught me several things about building confidence in myself. These were the most helpful:

Acknowledge the range of emotions I am feeling *now*. I will recognize them when they show up again in life. If I wanted to survive—indeed, thrive—in volatile and ever-changing environments, I needed to be able to land on my feet when confronted with other situations that are new and perhaps even more threatening.

As I began to feel the emotion in the future situations, I needed to get curious about how I could learn more about myself from it. If I mastered the emotion, I could solve the challenge and prevent lack of confidence from occurring again in the future.

I felt frustration that I couldn't perform push-ups like everyone else, anger at myself for not pushing harder before coming to the Academy, and embarrassment that I had not made a better impression on my new colleagues.

Remember a time when I felt a similar emotion and realize that I've successfully handled this emotion *in the past*. Since I've handled it before, I could do it again now.

I stopped and thought about other times I had felt little or no confidence in myself to accomplish the task at hand, and how I dealt with it in a positive way. I had difficulties, at times, in recollecting and instance when I had handled lack of confidence in a positive way. This is when I relied upon a journal to remind me. This is why journaling has been so important in helping me celebrate my successes. At the time, I was so busy just surviving that I didn't realize how I did it.

As I struggled to pass the FIT test at the FBI Academy, I reached back and thought about stacking hay bales during the hot summer months in Wyoming. We raised a lot of native hay on our meadows and my job was to help stack the bales into haystacks. Each bale weighed about fifty pounds and I had no trouble throwing them into place. If I did heavy lifting when I was a child, I could do it as an adult!

Feel certain I could handle the difficulty not only today, but also *in the future*. Simply remembering the way in which I handled this difficulty before helped me rehearse how I would handle something similar in the future.

Lack of confidence can hit us when making a presentation, talking with a stranger, or meeting with a supervisor. Prepare and rehearse so that you can reach back and retrieve past patterns of ways you've handled this emotion successfully.

When stacking bales of hay, or carrying log posts, or throwing a heavy saddle onto the back of a tall horse, I kept moving forward because there was no option. These were tasks that had to be done. This remembered mind-set gave me the confidence I could do whatever I set my mind to do. Somewhere along the way to the Academy, I had begun to doubt myself, and when that happened, I couldn't perform to the best of my ability.

I finally passed the physical fitness test and went on to work as an FBI agent for twenty-four years.

THINKING ABOUT CONFIDENCE

Points to Ponder: People will avoid the hard challenges in life because they have self-limiting beliefs about themselves.

Inspiration: *"Confidence is contagious. So is lack of confidence."*—Vince Lombardi

Reflection Questions: How have you felt confident in yourself?

We will look at three ways to help you build the strong mental muscles of confidence—small steps, use of questions, and mastery.

SMALL STEPS

"When you improve a little each day, eventually bigger things will come. Not tomorrow, not the next day, but eventually a big gain is made. Don't worry about short, quick improvements. Seek out the small improvements one day at a time. And when it happens—it lasts."

—JOHN WOODEN

As a case agent, I gave code names to the people I was investigating. I preferred ones that were easy to remember, based on some trait or characteristic that made them stand out in some way.

One of my more interesting subjects was a short, bald man in his early sixties who had begun to lose the battle of the bulge. He looked a lot like Fred Mertz from the popular nineteen fifties sitcom *I Love Lucy*. If he was Fred, then Olga, his wife, was Ethel.

Fred had been recruited by the KGB in the late 1960s after graduating from a Moscow university. We found out from other American intelligence agencies that Fred's father had been a KGB officer, which went a long way in explaining why such a well-disciplined organization like the KGB would have taken on the likes of Fred. The old boy network thrived in the Soviet Union and Fred's father had greased the skids for his son. Fred had risen to the rank of KGB colonel in spite of mediocre performance.

But now it was the late-1990s. The Soviet Union was now Russia, and the KGB was now the SVR.

Fred was not a ball of fire. He had the sort of work ethic that made the FBI wonder why San Francisco had become such a low priority for the KGB. Hostile intelligence services usually sent their top-rated officers to the Silicon Valley.

Fred was the sort of old-style Soviet who, after spending *three years* in San Francisco and wearing a suit every day, finally asked for the name of a dry cleaner.

There are a couple of ways to investigate a spy like Fred. One is to launch an aggressive investigation to identify, neutralize, and recruit. In the case of George (see chapter one), an ambitious man in the prime of building his operational portfolio, recruitment became the primary goal for the FBI. If the man worked so hard for Russia, it was a good bet he'd work as hard for the U.S.

We looked at Fred differently. While not the sharpest tool in the shed, he still had his finger on the pulse of SVR activities, particularly in San Francisco. The FBI already knew that by the late-nineties, the priorities in Silicon Valley had shifted from a narrow focus on classified military research to include economic and political intelligence as well. In short, FBI Headquarters and I decided not to recruit Fred—he would only be another load for the American taxpayer—but he had access to information valuable to the FBI.

I watched Fred and had him followed whenever he left the consulate. That was not often. Because his position was an internal one, he did not meet Americans or members of the Russian émigré community often. Fred was becoming a boring case. But one day, one of our surveillance units followed Ethel to a local discount clothing store.

One minute she was eyeing a shapeless, floral blouse and the next—it was gone! Ethel had shoved it into her cheap vinyl handbag. She then proceeded to the lingerie department where she found a size XXL girdle and did the same thing. We had a shoplifter on our hands.

Did Fred know? Our answer came about two months later when he accompanied his wife on one of her shopping trips. We had alerted the store of her arrival and worked with their security to follow their movements with a surveillance camera. The same thing happened, only this time Ethel stashed away items apparently meant for her grandchildren back in Russia. We caught everything on tape. They were both detained by store security on their way out.

He was shaken, she was not. She correctly pointed out to the security guard they were foreign diplomats and would be provided with diplomatic immunity. She could not be arrested and put in jail.

Store security immediately called the FBI and I was notified of the situation. I knew Fred would be hostile to an FBI interview at this time. We needed to move with small steps to ensure our footing was solid before taking the next one. I was also fairly certain that, when the right time came, he would view a female as less threatening since he was old-fashioned in his thinking. I thought this might work to my advantage.

I selected the biggest, tallest, toughest-looking male agent I could find from the bank robbery squad and asked him to accompany me to the department store. When we arrived, Ethel looked smug, but Fred looked worried. We all knew that, in order to get out of this mess, the San Francisco police would be called. They, in turn, would contact the Russian Consular Security Officer who, after hearing the charges, would confirm Fred's diplomatic status. The damage to Fred's already faltering reputation would be severe. He could be labeled a security risk and sent back to Russia.

The tough-looking bank robbery agent who accompanied me told Fred and Ethel that no charges would be filed—at this time—and no notification would be made to the Consulate's Security Officer. As we left, the agent leaned over to Fred and said, "We'll be in touch."

I talked the situation over with my supervisor. We let Fred stew for three days. Meanwhile, there was no indication that he had turned himself in to the Russian Consulate's Security Officer—another very important small step. We knew Fred was not confident enough in his position at the consulate to risk confiding his situation.

The tough-looking bank robbery agent and I waited until Fred was alone, driving in his car in the middle of the day. FBI agents drive unmarked cars, so I turned on our special headlights that flashed red and blue to signal law enforcement, and pulled him over to the side of the street. We then asked him to park his car behind a large apartment building and come with us.

He didn't protest or ask questions. He nodded curtly without making eye contact. Without saying a word, he sat in the back seat of the car with the bank robbery agent while I drove us to a small, private hotel near the beach.

We took the back stairs. Without speaking, Fred followed us to the hotel room. He sat down in a chair, back rigid, his toes apart, and his ankles locked. He clenched his hands together, making one massive fist, massaging one thumb against the other, and still refusing to make eye contact.

> At this point I felt it had become obvious that a female would be perceived as less threatening, and perhaps, less competent. This was a time to let sexism work. So I sat down in the chair opposite Fred while my colleague remained standing.

I introduced my colleague and myself in true name. I explained that the FBI had no desire to endanger either his life or his career, and because of that, I had no intention of asking him to work for the FBI. In some situations like this, the FBI would pressure the spy to return to Moscow and remain in his current position. This would allow the spy to meet with U.S. intelligence officers several times during the year with information on operations abroad and in the U.S.

No one is recruited who doesn't truly want to be. There have been a few instances of blackmailing to coerce cooperation, but such situations are few and seldom productive in the long term.

Fred could be blackmailed at this point, but his surly attitude guaranteed resentment and threatened to pollute the information he would provide. If he could get even, he would, and this was not a good way to start a relationship.

I told Fred that we had no desire for him to work for the U.S. government. In fact, we did not even want any further prolonged contact with him. I waited as a little bead of perspiration burst and ran in a rivulet down his temple and into his shirt collar. His breathing returned to normal, he looked at me, and with dry lips, asked, "What are you after?" I already knew his English was good and that communication would not be a problem, although I had a translator in a nearby room in case he stalled for time by pretending he didn't understand his situation. When he spoke, I noticed several of his front teeth were capped in gold, a symbol of privilege under the old Soviet system.

"I want about eight hours of your time," I replied. "I want you to identify every intelligence officer in the consulate, both SVR and military GRU. I also want a rundown of their operations."

In short, all I wanted from Fred was a data dump. In return, not only would I tear up the shoplifting report and give him the store surveillance tape, I would deposit several thousands of dollars into any account he wanted. I'd give it to him in cash if he preferred.

Fred said yes to the cash.

Foreign diplomats are given diplomatic immunity. This means they can, and do, frequently break American laws knowing they cannot be arrested and prosecuted—those crimes frequently include shoplifting, parking violations, and speeding tickets. Any deal cut with Fred would not include Ethel's illegal activities. It is common practice, however, for either the FBI or local police department to notify the consulate or embassy of the offense. As a matter of courtesy and on-going diplomatic relations, the offending diplomats are usually censored internally. In some cases, if the offense is egregious enough, they are sent back to their home country.

ANATOMY OF A SEDUCTION

The word *seduction* is something you pay attention to, but the seduction *process* is something you rarely notice.

The reason is that seduction is a series of small steps—steps so small you're unaware of them happening. Persuading a foreign spy to work for the FBI is very similar to wooing a lover, it begins with a series of small steps.

A seduction is a series of small movements toward the goal. The reason small achievements are so successful is because they are believable. You gain confidence every time you move forward.

Small, steady steps made it possible for the FBI to craft a successful approach to Fred. We believed that he had braced himself for a blackmail approach wherein he would be given no option other than cooperate or risk being exposed and sent back to Moscow as a security risk. His career—and pension—would be in ruins.

Fred was not expecting the situation to move in the direction that it did. As a result, he was not prepared. His mind was so focused on blackmail that when another, less onerous option was presented, he grabbed it and thought it a good bargain at that!

Fred committed treason, just as surely as if he had handed over classified documents. But small steps softened the blow to the point that Fred was able to justify his actions in his own conscience. Small steps allowed the FBI to move slow enough we could be certain of his response before we made our proposal.

Little things that made Fred feel uncomfortable about his situation and not in control included:

Introducing him to a burly FBI agent at the department store that fit his stereotype of what an agent looked like.

Throwing the small sentence to him as the FBI agent was leaving, "We'll be in touch."

Allowing him to stew about his situation for three days before confronting him.

Little things that made Fred feel more comfortable about his situation included:

Using a younger agent to negotiate, giving him confidence he was more senior, and therefore, smarter.

Using a female agent to negotiate, giving him even more confidence he could handle the situation.

Asking him for eight hours of his time instead of eight months, or eight years, gave him hope that the mess would be over very soon.

All these little things influenced Fred's decision to cooperate with the FBI. In fact, we believe he left confident that the FBI had not fully exploited his unfortunate situation and that he had struck a good deal. My experience with Fred taught me that change can happen in a minute—if you prepare with small steps.

THINKING ABOUT SMALL STEPS

Point to Ponder: Small steps can lead to big changes.

Inspiration: *"I forgot that every little action of the common day makes or unmakes character."*—Oscar Wilde (from his prison cell).

Reflection Question: What small steps have made a difference for you?

QUESTIONS

"A wise man can learn more from a foolish question than a fool can learn from a wise answer."

—BRUCE LEE

I learned the importance of asking the right questions from a Russian man I met while trying to identify the activities of a Russian delegation visiting from St. Petersburg.

A foreign intelligence service had alerted us to the fact that one of the delegate members was observed meeting with a known SVR officer in another country prior to entry into the United States. Alex's name came up as one of those who had sponsored the delegation. I called for an interview and met one of the most amazing men I've ever had the privilege of knowing.

Alex was born in 1920, and when eighteen years of age, he was conscripted into the Russian army. He fought in WWII, and early in the war, the Germans captured Alex with five other Russian soldiers. Neither Alex nor his Russian comrades could speak German, so they couldn't communicate properly with the guards. German guards took all six to a wooden barrack with two double doors secured with a lock and chain. A guard stood on either side of the doors and when Alex was brought up, one of the guards placed a key inside the lock and unchained the doors. To make room for the six new prisoners, six of the weakest prisoners standing in the front line were pulled out, taken aside, and shot.

Alex learned quickly that, if he wanted to survive, he would have to shove his way to the back of the barrack. Those not strong enough were pushed forward until the day when the door opened and they were the weak ones in the front line. Each day, enough prisoners were shot to make room for incoming ones. The barracks held prisoners of war from many countries and many dialects. The prisoners were asking questions like, "Will I die?" "Who else speaks my language?" "How can we plan an escape when no one understands each other?" "How could I have been captured? What went wrong?"

Alex asked a different question of himself. "How can I survive in this hostile, volatile, and ever changing environment?" He immediately got his answer. Little by little over the next few months, Alex learned enough German to understand and speak the language.

The prisoners existed on a meager diet of stale bread and watered down soup. Each day Alex weakened until one day he found himself on the front line. Eight new prisoners were brought in that day, and when the guards opened the double doors, Alex was the first person they saw. Too weak to resist when pulled outside, he looked at the guard and asked in German, "Why are you shooting prisoners of war?"

"You are Jewish first, and prisoners of war second," the guard said. Alex replied in German, "I am not Jewish." The guard wouldn't believe him. Finally, Alex dropped his pants. "I am NOT Jewish. Take me to another barrack." The guard, upon seeing that Alex was not circumcised, gesticulated to the other guards and after minutes of discussion, Alex was moved to another barrack.

The difference between Alex and the other prisoners of war in that barrack was that Alex asked a different question. As a result, he saved his life. That same instinct to make decisions by asking the right questions stayed with Alex until he was liberated by the Americans in 1945 and came to America where he began a new life as a janitor. Other immigrants and refugees asked, "How can I find a job and support my family?" Alex asked, "How can I help the owner of this business?" He became a trusted employee, and twenty years later, Alex was the Chief Operating Officer of one of the largest companies in the city.

> Alex was always confident in his ability to land on his feet regardless of his situation. He asked difficult questions because he was confident he could handle the answers. Even if the answers demanded a lot of work and sacrifice, he moved forward with confidence that he would find a way to survive.

Alex is a remarkable example of how a person can change his destiny by asking the right questions. He used them to evaluate and enlarge his understanding of his environment. He was successful throughout his life because he had the confidence to ask the better questions, and as a result, got the better answers. His answers were better because each one empowered him to understand how to react in different situations that faced him in business and life.

IF YOU WANT A GREAT LIFE, ASK A GREAT QUESTION

Questions can be catalysts that hint at something better to be found in us.

They are challenges, inspirations, and road maps to the future. It takes time to excavate the significance of our own stories and experiences. Most of us find our past experiences help us to recall how our resilience got us through the tough times.

The power of our own stories and experiences can encourage us to move beyond the limits we set around ourselves. Questions can be a magic wand that probes deeply into our mind. Questions are entry points into significant conversations about issues, values, and goals that are most important to us. If you want to start a significant conversation, ask a significant question. The questions do not have to be brilliant or well crafted; instead, they need to be from the heart and wrapped in genuine curiosity.

BE CURIOUS

Here are two things about building confidence through the power of questions that I learned from Alex:

Questions can change your focus. Alex did not see himself as a victim of his circumstances. The questions he asked of himself created confidence that he could, and therefore *would*, find a way to overcome his dire situation. He did not ask, "Why me?"

Instead, he asked, "How can I change my situation?" This question changed the focus of his attention, and his energies followed the new direction of his attention—confidence that he could find a way to survive.

Changing your focus is not a passive process. You see exactly what you expect to see. Stereotypes and generalizations can impede your ability to see your situation clearly. If you are aware of this, you are better able to choose the way you react to your ever-changing environment.

A few years ago, a man sat at a metro station in Washington DC and started to play the violin. It was a cold January morning. He played six Bach pieces for about 45 minutes. During that time, since it was rush hour, it was calculated that thousands of people went through the station.

One man stopped for a few seconds and then hurried on to meet his schedule. A little later, a woman threw a dollar into the hat and without stopping continued on her way. When he finished playing and silence took over, no one noticed it. No one applauded, nor was there any recognition. The violinist was Joshua Bell, one of the best musicians in the world. He played one of the most intricate pieces ever written and on a violin worth 3.5 million dollars. Two days before his playing in the subway, Joshua Bell sold out at a theater in Boston where the cost of the seats averaged $100.

The Washington Post arranged to have Joshua Bell play incognito in the metro station as part of a social experiment. Because he was playing in a subway station, people assumed he was a street musician playing for handouts and paid little attention to his music. People saw and heard what they expected to see and hear from a street musician. German guards saw and heard what they expected to see from a man they believed to be Jewish. This did not deter Alex. He changed his focus, away from that of a prisoner with little hope of survival, to that of an individual determined to find a way out of his circumstances. When he changed his focus, he transformed the context of his situation.

Questions can change your attitude. Alex was one of the most optimistic people I've ever met, in spite of an experience that would have left many others in his situation depressed or angry. He would not allow his attitude to become negative, because if he did, he would have ceased to be curious about his environment. If this happened, he would have given up. A positive attitude is directly linked to confidence in one's abilities to overcome obstacles.

Researchers at John Hopkins University[8] found that lawyers suffered from depression at a rate of 3.6 times higher than people employed in other professions. Training your mind to look for errors and problems, in careers like law or accounting, can lead you toward a pessimism that carries over into your personal life.

Is there a way to get your mind out of these negative loops? Yes. Train your brain to change your attitude and seek out the good things in life. Do this by giving yourself the time to explore your thoughts and relive your positive memories.

Good questions need to be made with intentionality, otherwise you may settle for something that is second best without ever realizing when you took the wrong turn in the road. If you are looking for questions that will give you the confidence to change direction in your life, the answers must come from inside.

THE PURPOSE OF A GREAT QUESTION

Judge a person by their questions rather than by their answers. The secret of an FBI stealth interrogation is never to ask direct questions. Instead, come at them from the side, a tactic that uncovers the interviewee's hidden concerns.

Here are some types of effective questions based on my FBI training:

Open-Ended. If you're looking for insight or information, never ask a question that can be answered by a yes or no. Questions that begin with *do*, *would*, or *could* all invite a monosyllable answer. Instead, ask open-ended questions that begin with *how*, *what*, or *why*.

Specific. Focus on the area of concern by asking specific questions, not vague ones. Notice words that are freighted with feeling or energy because they have more meaning to the person who is talking. Once you hear one of those words, follow up with an open-ended question. For example, in one of our conversations Fred said, "Isn't this just in the FBI's bag of *tricks*?" I felt an emphasis on the word "tricks." He was afraid we were not making him a legitimate offer, so I asked, "Bag of tricks?" This left Fred explaining what a trick would look like to him. I was then able to address his specific concern in language he understood.

Paced. If we're accustomed to having all the answers, we can get uncomfortable with periods of silence. Rapid-fire questions are exhausting—for everyone. Moments of reflection in any conversation can be productive.

Polite. Good manners matter. Showing respect for the other person is the single most important thing you can do for them. The questions you ask should be presented in a respectful and polite manner.

Focused. Good questions are goal-oriented. Be clear about your goals before you begin because it will be much easier to frame your question. Understand why you're asking a question before you ask it. Open-ended questions can be focused, but don't ask ones that can be answered "yes" or "no."

Honest. Manipulation is akin to extortion—it may get you what you want, once, but it doesn't build long-term relationships. Transparency in the type of questions you are asking will get better results.

Not Judgmental. If you want honest answers, make certain you don't come across as confrontational or judgmental. Let the other person feel that they've been heard and respected.

By asking the right questions, you can uncover the wants, fears, and interests of others and achieve better communication skills.

THINKING ABOUT QUESTIONS

Point to Ponder: Great questions have powerful answers.

Inspiration: *"At the end of the day, the questions we ask of ourselves determine the type of people we will become."*—Leo Babauta

Reflection Question: What is the best question you've ever been asked?

MASTERY

"Desire is the starting point of all achievement, not a hope, not a wish, but a keen pulsating desire that transcends everything."

—NAPOLEAN HILL

The best way to gain confidence is by becoming very good at doing the thing you want to do.

I had never shot a gun in my life before arriving at the FBI Academy. My dad had a lot of guns around the house but I had never been interested in learning how to shoot. The firearms instructors liked that I hadn't been taught how to handle a gun the "wrong" way, which meant anything other than the FBI way.

My first weapon was a 357 Smith and Wesson .38 caliber revolver. It had a three-inch barrel and held six rounds at a time, each round loaded into the chamber by hand. By the time I graduated from the Academy, I had shot over three thousand rounds of ammunition. Our first qualifying firearms course started at the fifty-yard line. If you've never shot a three-inch barrel gun from that distance, believe me when I say that it's hard to hit the target.

I was a good shot from twenty-five yards and closer, but hitting all twelve rounds of ammunition from the fifty-yard line was a challenge. It was a cool spring day and I remember standing up after shooting and looking down to see dark spots on a target—I had several hits! I was excited, and ran down with the others to check my score after we'd holstered our guns. Alas, I found my dark spots to be nothing more than flecks of mud that splattered on my target where I'd shot into the rain soaked ground.

After the mud incident, I was not confident in my ability to shoot a gun and hit my target. I continued to shoot my revolver every day for four months. The soft flesh at the base of my thumb became bruised from the recoil. At times I wondered how the firearms exercises, in addition to the problem-solving scenarios, would help me become a better, or more effective, FBI Agent. But mastery with a gun, I knew, would give me confidence in my ability to carry out my duties as an FBI agent authorized to carry a weapon.

As my FBI training progressed, I learned there is a connection between mastery, confidence, and discomfort zones.

FBI counselors and instructors made certain our lives were surrounded with volatile and changing environments so they structured uncertainty into the curriculum. The reason? The unknown throws us off center and moves us out of our comfort zone. When it does, it's up to us to decide how to land on our feet. It's as much about confidence in our personal strengths as it is about talent and muscles.

DISCOMFORT ZONES

The world is becoming more competitive.

The trend toward achievement in most areas of life is toward higher performance and more competition. The winner of the men's 200-meter race in the 1908 Olympics ran it in 22.6 seconds;

today's high school record is faster by more than 2 seconds. When Tchaikovsky finished writing his violin concerto in 1878, he was told that the piece was too complicated and unplayable; today, violinists graduating from Julliard can play it. The game of chess is being played today at a much higher level than it was in the nineteenth century.

There is immense pressure for people to perform at higher standards and develop their own abilities than was ever necessary before. Therefore, any information about what can make us better at what we want to do can be used to make us more effective and happier.

> **If you are to believe the theory that it takes approximately 10 years or 10,000 hours of practice to become a master, why aren't there more of them?**

Most of the people you know spend hours every day, month, and year at their work. Clearly, they've put in the time, and yet how many of them are great performers in their field? Even after years of education and hard work, the hard truth is that very few people will ever become a master or achieve greatness.

In fact, while many people perform their jobs at a perfectly acceptable level, they not only fail at becoming a master in their chosen profession, they never actually become even good at it. It is easier to dismiss great performers as those who have a God-given talent that they discovered in early childhood. We are told that this explains the success of Tiger Woods, Tchaikovsky, or Mozart.

It's not that simple. You may assume that outstanding performers have outstanding intelligence. Some do, but many do not. Some international chess masters have below average IQ's. Whatever it is that makes these people special, it isn't superhuman capabilities. The factor that differentiates great performers from the rest is deliberate practice. This calls for more than just showing up every day at work or even getting good grades.

The FBI was training me to be a master in firearms through deliberate practice. The definition of mastery is performing the same task time and time again with near perfect results each time. This meant I needed to be mentally and psychologically engaged each time I picked up my revolver and aimed it at a target. By the time I graduated from the Academy, I had become a master marksman by shooting in the high nineties in every target practice.

> Deliberate practice is exhausting because it requires the mental discipline of concentration and the physical discipline of continual hard work. It is not just showing up, it is showing up with the specific intention of becoming a master in your field.

You may assume that others may be more talented than you, and therefore will be more of a success. If you were a pianist who lived during the time of Amadeus Wolfgang Mozart, you would find yourself overshadowed by his genius. If however, you looked more closely at the life of Mozart, you would find that his father, Leopold, was a pianist and a domineering parent who started Wolfgang in intensive training at the age of three. Leopold Mozart was a backstage father determined to see his son succeed.

Many of Wolfgang's early compositions were not in his own hand but in that of his father. By the time Wolfgang had composed his masterpiece Piano Concerto No. 9, he was twenty-one. That is an early age, but it's important to remember that he had been through eighteen years of extremely hard, expert training. Although Wolfgang was talented, he worked hard to become a master. There are other examples in business as well.

At one point, John D. Rockefeller was the richest man in the world. He was described as forgettable and undistinguishable from other students. In fact, one former teacher of Rockefeller later recalled, "I have no recollection of John excelling at anything. But I do remember that he worked very hard at everything."

Mozart's genius and Rockefeller's success were the product of deliberate practice and old-fashioned hard work. Great performance takes more than experience, does not need to be an innate ability, and cannot be measured against intelligence.

MOVE FORWARD WITH DELIBERATE STEPS

Firearms proficiency was the result of deliberate practice at the Academy.

Once I had mastered how to handle my weapon, I was confident in my ability to use it. These are lessons I learned from my firearms training:

Improvement. High achievers are constantly looking for ways to stretch themselves beyond their current abilities. Most adults put in an incredible amount of work repeating exactly what they've been doing for the past several years. Deliberate practice[9], on the other hand, requires the identification of specific elements of the performance that need to be improved, and then work intently on them. To become a master at anything almost always requires the help of a coach or teacher because very few people can make a clear, honest assessment of their own performance.

Repetition. Repeating a specific activity over and over is what most of us mean by practice. Deliberate practice takes it to the next step. It is repeating activities in which we need improvement until we can accomplish them at high volume with near perfect results each and every time.

Mental challenge. Deliberate practice requires a tremendous amount of focus and concentration. This is what makes it deliberate as opposed to unintentional. Continually seeking those elements of performance that are unsatisfactory and then trying our hardest to make them better places a great deal of mental stress on us.

No fun. Doing things we know how to do well is fun. Deliberate practice, however, demands that we continually move into the discomfort zone and intentionally seek out what we are *not* good at—when we identify the painful, difficult activities that will make us better and do them over and over again. With each repetition, we continue to repeat the most painful and difficult elements of the performance until we've mastered them.

People who become masters do not believe that there are limits to their performance. The difference between expert performers and average performers is a life-long deliberate effort to improve performance in their area of expertise.

DAVID AND GOLIATH

The Old Testament story of David fighting Goliath[10] is a story of confidence and mastery.

David was a sheepherder whose safe and predictable world was thrown into chaos when he was chosen by God to be a leader of the Israelites. The Philistine army had gathered their troops for war against Israel. The two armies faced each other, camped for battle on opposite sides of a steep valley. Every day for forty days, a Philistine warrior named Goliath broke out from the front line and challenged the Israelites to fight. Goliath was reported to be a giant—he measured over nine feet tall—and wore full armor.

Described as a runt by his father, David's job was to run back and forth from herding sheep to bring news of his brothers who were all on the Israelite battle line. Following his father's orders, David had left food for his brothers and was preparing to return to tending his flock when he heard Goliath's war cry.

The Israelites fell back in fear when they saw the huge form of Goliath challenging them. David asked, "What's in it for the man who kills that ugly Philistine?" When he learned that King Saul would offer a huge reward and give his daughter in marriage, David volunteered to fight Goliath.

The soldiers laughed at David because he did not have a soldier's training. The first thing that the army tried to do was turn David into one of them. They suited him up in their armor and gave him a sword. But David was not a soldier and he had never trained as one. He said, "I cannot walk in these because I'm not used to them." The techniques and skills of a soldier were not his own, and he was wise enough to acknowledge what he didn't know so he could focus on what he did. When David met Goliath on the battlefield, he reached into his bag and slung one of his stones at the hole in the armor that protected Goliath's head. The giant fell face down on the ground.

David understood that he would excel only by maximizing his strengths and not by trying to fix his weaknesses. Far from ignoring his weaknesses, he simply acknowledged them so he could manage them and free up his time to focus on his strengths.

David's mastery with a slingshot gave him confidence that he could defeat Goliath. He'd go after lions and bears when they carried off lambs, knocking them down and rescuing the lamb. They were big and strong opponents—as big and strong as Goliath—but if the bear or lion turned on him, he'd use his skill with a slingshot to kill it.

David was confident he could kill Goliath because he knew how to protect lambs from large and strong predators and he was prepared to use those same skills to protect the Israelites. Mastery as a sheepherder protecting his herd demanded that David remain focused and dedicated to his goal. It had taken years of practice, but he had never become distracted from learning the skills he needed to become a master of his trade. He had learned lessons about tenacity, dealing with change, and overcoming fierce obstacles in his job as a shepherd.

He met Goliath on the battlefield with a slingshot and five smooth stones because those were the tools of his trade. He had used these same tools against lions and bears. From the outside, he looked like an underdog. From David's point of view, however, he possessed a strong mind as well as a strong arm and understood how to adapt to his circumstances. He used the skills and talents given to him by God.

People who become masters do not believe that there are various limits that they simply will not get past. The difference between expert performers and normal adults is a life-long deliberate effort to improve performance in their area of expertise.

THINKING ABOUT MASTERY

Points to Ponder: Mastery demands all from a person.
Inspiration: *"If people knew how hard I worked to get my mastery, it wouldn't seem so wonderful at all."*—Michelangelo
Reflection Questions: How do you know when you've mastered something?

CONFIDENCE TACTICS

SMALL STEPS

Here are some ways you can take small steps to overcome an obstacle:

Recall a major mistake that you've made at some point in your life. Now, take time to consider whether there were small signs along the way that indicated things were not going according to your plan. Did you ignore the small problems and hope they'd go away? Did you take actions to correct the problem?

Identify a small mistake you've made recently. Don't become angry with yourself. Just acknowledge how you became aware of it.

Does the small mistake you identified above reflect a larger problem? Does it have the potential to gather momentum? By simply paying attention to this mistake, you will reduce the likelihood that you'll make it again.

Ask yourself if there are small ways that you irritate your colleagues, family members, or friends. Your new awareness of ways you irritate them reduces the probability that you will do it again. If you link your behavior to their reaction, you've already begun to work on eliminating it.

"When I face the desolate impossibility of writing 500 pages, a sick sense of failure falls on me, and I know I can never do it. Then gradually, I write one page and then another. One day's work is all I can permit myself to contemplate."

—JOHN STEINBECK

QUESTIONS

The right question can change your entire outlook on life.

CHANGE OF FOCUS QUESTIONS:

What is something *new* that I observed today?

What is something *new* that that I experienced this week?

What would I like to accomplish in the next 12 months?

What do I need to do today to make that happen?

CHANGE OF ATTITUDE QUESTIONS:

Who is the happiest person I know?

Who are the people I like and respect the most? Why?

What are three *new* things I am thankful for each day?

Can I describe one positive experience I've had each day?

CHANGE OF DIRECTIONS QUESTIONS:

What do I truly love?

What am I good at?

What brings me satisfaction?

What was the road I did not take in life?

Is that road still beckoning me?

What would that road look like today if I did take it?

MASTERY

Here are two strategies that can help you gain the confidence to achieve mastery:

1. LEAVE THE FAMILIAR. Moving into unknown territory can seem scary because the path is not illuminated. You're not sure what you might encounter. You might stumble and make mistakes—but your world will never get bigger until you find ways to enlarge it, and this means moving out of the familiar.

As a baby, you do not want to leave the comforts of the womb. You came kicking and screaming, and often continue these habits any time you enter a new life experience.

New agents spend 16 weeks isolated at the FBI Academy. At first I thought this was to build team spirit. It was, to some degree, but more importantly, it was to prevent us from running away—from ourselves. There was nowhere to go, except inward. Here is what I learned about leaving the familiar:

√ **Embarking upon uncharted territory means making mistakes** – no one is perfect at everything. Embrace mistakes in the company of others doing the same thing and you'll feel more like taking risks.

√ **Re-examine self-image** – our self-perception may not be accurate or it may be based on false assumptions. Once you learn to draw out what is new and challenging, you will know which self-images are accurate and which ones are not.

2. LET GO OF EGO. Mastery is about learning—from everything about yourself to the situation in which you find yourself. Society has told you that to be successful you must have the answers. The more you know, the more intelligent and competent you are seen to be. This feeds the ego, which is why letting go of the ego is the most difficult strategy to incorporate. Until you are willing to be a beginner, there is very little you can learn.

Ego can be a tremendous impediment to achieving the truly difficult things in life because you don't want to admit you don't know everything. Here are some ways to let go of ego:

√ **Resist the temptation to complain** – ego strengthens itself by complaining

√ **Avoid negative reactions** – grievances and resentments are a way to punish others

√ **Forget about being right** – the ego loves to be right

√ **Embrace your weaknesses and fears** – the ego tries to blame others for our imperfections

Achieving mastery in your area of expertise, feeling comfortable with small steps, and becoming adept with asking the right questions of yourself and others will give you the confidence to move into discomfort zones. Now, all it will take is determination.

CHAPTER 5

DETERMINATION

"Success is a little like wrestling a gorilla. You don't quit when you're tired. You quit when the gorilla is tired."

—ROBERT STRAUSS

One of the final physical fitness requirements at the FBI Academy was to dive off a 25-foot diving board while holding an M16 rifle, and then swim to the other side of the pool with the gun. I had two problems: I was afraid of heights, and I had never learned to swim.

As my training class and instructors waited for me to jump, I seriously doubted that in real life I'd ever need to jump into a pool of water with a M16 while chasing a suspect. I didn't find out about this requirement until about two weeks into the Academy but it was something I had to do, however, to graduate.

Everything in the FBI Academy is alphabetical, so I was one of the last. I watched as even the experienced swimmers came up gagging and gasping for breath. All of my attention and energy was taken up with this single question: How can I do this? How can I jump, bounce to the top, and swim to the other side? I knew that intense fear can dull one's other senses.

Only when it was my time to climb the diving board, did I tell an instructor I couldn't' swim. He was incredulous. He got me a life vest and we strapped it on. I could see the doubt in his eyes as he handed me the M16: Can she do this?

I didn't know either. First, I had to climb the steps.

After I managed to do that, and then looked down from the top of the diving board, the water was clear and calm. I could see not only down 25-feet to the water, but to the bottom of the pool—another 10-feet! I remained gripped with fear. If I took that step off the diving board, I would die. I would find myself at the bottom of the pool, take a deep breath, and my lungs would immediately fill with water.

> If I did not take that step, I would not graduate from the FBI Academy. My determination to become an FBI Agent was greater than my fear of water or heights.

I knew what determination looked like; I'd seen my Dad jump into a flooding river to save a drowning calf. He moved toward the conflict; in doing so, he moved toward the unknown.

At some point, up on that diving board, I heard the cheers from my classmates, and when a couple of them jumped back into the pool to encourage me, I knew I could do it. I could move toward the unknown. I took a step and jumped. When I went into the water, instinct took over and I bounced back up to the surface—still holding the gun—and then floundered until I made the other side. I hadn't been overcome with an overwhelming need to breathe under water.

My jump and swim had not been pretty, but I managed to claw my way to the steps where my instructors waited for me.

It wasn't until a few years later that I realized the swimming pool test had nothing to do with superior law enforcement techniques. Instead, it taught agents in training that only by falling into the unknown would we be able to explore it.

To increase safety, move toward the unknown. To increase chances for success, move toward the challenge.

The closer we get to the unknown, the more we can educate ourselves about it. The steps to follow and actions to take may not reveal themselves to us until we have moved closer to the situation. To deepen our understanding of determination, let's explore its three key components: willpower, flexibility, and persistence. If willpower and flexibility get us to our destination, persistence will keep us there.

THINKING ABOUT DETERMINATION

Points to Ponder: Determination dictates how you deal with upsets and challenges.

Inspiration: *"Determination is the wake-up call to the human will."*—Anthony Robbins

Reflection Question: What is your best example of being determined?

WILLPOWER

"Strength does not come from physical capacity. It comes from an indomitable will."

—MAHATMA GANDHI

The swimming pool was not my first frightening encounter with water ...

When I was twelve years old, I helped my dad herd twenty cows and their calves across the flooding North Laramie River. It was spring and the winter snow was thawing, causing the riverbanks to overflow. We were moving the small bunch to join the rest of the herd on the west meadow.

We decided to herd the cattle across the river at a shallow point. In the summer this area was low enough to drive a pickup through so we knew there was no danger of a cow drowning. The river quickly narrowed into rapids, however, as it ran downhill and into deeper depths where the ice chunks moved more languidly. I knew these areas were deep holes dug out by swirling water. I stayed away from them because I couldn't swim. Even in the height of summer, the water melting from Laramie Peak never reached above 60 degrees—too cold for me!

This was the first time I'd helped trail cattle across a flooding river. Sitting on the back of my horse, Buckshot, while crossing fast moving water was a strange sensation. I got disoriented and it felt as though Buckshot was caught up in the current and moving toward the rapids. I couldn't tell whether we were going sideways or forwards. I knew that if we got caught in the rapids,

Buckshot wouldn't be able to stay on his feet. If I fell off, I'd be quickly swept into a deep hole and drown.

Out of panic, I pulled up on the reins. Buckshot and I stood in the middle of the flooding river. I could feel the churning, muddy ice water just below my stirrup. Dad shouted at me to keep moving because some of the calves were so small they had to swim. I kept my eye on a tree on the other side of the river so I wouldn't become dizzy. Buckshot was steady on his feet, took his time, and didn't stumble. I was useless as a helper, though, because I wasn't watching the calves.

All of a sudden, I heard a bellow and turned to see a calf starting to drift downstream with the water. I froze. Instead of trying to get around him to help orientate him so he could move in the same direction as the rest of the herd, I pulled up on the reins again and watched. All I could think about was how easy it would be for Buckshot and me to get caught in the rapids and end up drowning in the deep hole.

> I continued to watch as the calf drifted
> quickly through the rapids and began
> floundering. I knew he would drown and
> could see the panic in his wild, scared eyes.

I felt shame and embarrassment that I was doing nothing to help, but was too afraid to do anything other than watch. I don't remember hearing a thing, but I'm sure there must have been shouting and splashing. My dad, however, did not hesitate. He kicked his horse, a gray gelding named Man O'War, into action.

Both of them plunged into the water after the calf. With one hand on his saddle horn and the other on his rope, he tried to throw a lasso around the calf's head. It took a couple of attempts, and Man O'War also seemed to panic in the cold water surrounded by flowing chunks of ice, but stayed near the calf. Eventually dad was able to throw a rope around the calf and haul it to the riverbank.

Dad never learned to swim, either, so his life was in as much danger as the calf's. As I watched, I realized he could have as easily drown as the animal whose life he was trying to save, but he did not hesitate to go after it. There were two reasons I knew of: one, seeing a young animal drown would be horrible to witness; second, we raised cattle for a living and dad was saving a part of his business when he jumped into the river.

Dad had good old-fashioned willpower. Willpower is the determination to accomplish a goal despite fierce obstacles.

WILLPOWER IS TRUE GRIT

Willpower is sustained interest in long-term goals.

My dad's long-term goal was to sell his cattle at market in the fall. To do this, he needed as many calves as possible to prosper through the summer. Willpower is the ability to keep going in the face of difficulties. Often, it also means taking the tougher strategy rather than ones that are easier and more rewarding. Taking the tougher road can pay off, especially when things get hard. It's not strategy that helps people like my dad win; it's the willpower that is the bridge between strategy and performance.

People with willpower know that success is more than talent. If you think that your ability is due to talent, you will give up when you hit a wall. On the other hand, if you believe your ability has to do with effort, when you hit a problem you will refocus your efforts. If you have willpower, you will seek out challenges, take tougher strategies, and keep plugging along when things get hard.

Willpower has value for people at all levels of ability. West Point Military Academy spends thousands of dollars on each student who enrolls, but as many as five percent of these new cadets drop out so West Point had a financial motivation to find ways to predict attrition. A questionnaire that was administered to the 2008 new cadets revealed that willpower is the single best indicator for predicting which cadets would survive West Point's first weeks. It proved to be more reliable than SAT scores, athletic experience, or IQ tests[11].

Sticking it out through fierce and volatile conditions has less to do with how smart you are and more to do with your character. Attitude is more important than facts. The determination to keep moving forward depends a great deal upon the thoughts that continually occupy your mind.

HOW TO DEVELOP WILLPOWER

Here are four steps I took to develop willpower to burst through barriers:

Discover and understand goals. From years of working and living on a cattle ranch, I loved animals and wanted to rescue them from inhumane treatment. As a child, I thought about becoming a game warden so I could track down poachers and others who exploited defenseless animals.

Only after I interviewed with the FBI, did I realize that I had widened my goals over time. My desire for justice now also included people, and not just animals, that were victimized.

Connect personal willpower with a larger vision. If my goal was to become an FBI agent, my vision was about something greater than myself— I knew I wanted to do something that would make a difference in the world.

My ultimate goal must be about something greater than me. My willpower had its roots in my personal goals and dreams; however, my effectiveness as a leader depended on my ability to inspire and motivate others. People would want to follow my cause only if they could see that I was working on something meaningful. If I could link my personal and professional goals, I could decide where to use willpower to break through the important barriers.

Acquire the skills needed to achieve goals. I turned to my physical fitness coach for the skills I needed to pass the Academy's FIT test.

As I looked down from the diving board, I relived the terror I felt as I rode Buckshot across the flooding North Laramie River.

Having allowed myself to become paralyzed with fear that day, I was determined it wouldn't happen to me again.

Much of my mental toughness came from remembering how I'd used it in the past when confronted with volatile or hostile situations—like the charging bull or riding my nasty pony, Socks. My FBI training at the Academy continued to hone and clarify my personal strengths by moving me out of my comfort zone and forcing me to break through barriers. If I continued to worry about what was left out, I'd overlook the strengths that were left in.

Enlist the aid of both friend and foe. There were times at the Academy when I looked at my coaches as the enemy! They were yelling in my ear every day. And because all my new agent class-mates had outperformed me in physical fitness, I did not always feel charitable toward them, either. In fact, I noticed from high on that diving board that several of them walked out when they thought I was not going to jump from the diving board. As I stood on that diving board and watched them leave, their doubt in me only made me more determined to jump. Later, they came up and congratulated me and apologized. I accepted their apology.

MOVE TOWARD THE THREAT

Remember David and Goliath from the previous chapter?

I talked about how David's ability to master his skills with a slingshot gave him the confidence to confront Goliath, the

Philistine giant. There is one other lesson we can learn from this story. According to the Biblical account, "David took off from the front line, running toward the Philistine." David took leadership of the situation when he broke the pattern of the challenge. He moved toward the threat and pressed into the unknown.

Only by moving closer to the threat was David able to see where and how to strike. Opportunities that could not be seen from a distance were made visible as he pressed forward.

The closer Goliath came, the more ways David could see of defeating the giant. He saw a small hole in Goliath's armor that was not visible from a distance. As Goliath moved in for the kill, David reached into his bag and slung one of his stones at the hole in the armor that protected Goliath's head. The giant fell face down on the ground. David then took Goliath's own sword, killed him, and cut off his head. When the Philistines saw that their hero was dead, they turned and ran.

David would not have seen the small hole in Goliath's armor if he had not moved closer to the threat. There are other examples of how moving ahead provides clarity—a rugged mountain with sheer cliffs looks impossible to climb from a distance. Mountain climbers cannot plan how they will place their hands and feet on the mountain until they get closer to see crevices and footholds. They do not need total clarity as they begin their climb; they just need a goal and the determination to put one foot in front of the other.

When confronted with changing environments and fierce challenges, you may need to leave your place of safety and press forward with the willpower of a strong mind. Nothing is impossible. It's up to you to find a way. Even the most prepared and effective leaders can find themselves in a volatile environment where plans have failed and they need to lean into their natural strengths and a strong mind to survive.

WILLPOWER IS FOR SPRINTS, NOT MARATHONS

Willpower is a limited resource.

You only have a certain amount of willpower. It burns out quickly, but if directed with intention, it can provide you with the burst you need to move forward. Think of it as a specific attack rather than an entire battle. Willpower is a concentration of force. You gather up all of your energy and make a massive strike. Attack your problems at their weakest points until they crack and allow you to move deeper into their territory so you can finish them off.

Willpower strategy includes the following:

Identify a specific barrier preventing you from achieving your goal.

Attack the barrier by the "smooth handle." Take hold of it from the angle that will allow you the most control initially.

Draw close and hold on until you can see where next to move.

Willpower is unsustainable, so use it wisely. If you attempt to use it for too long, you'll burn out. The question naturally arises: If willpower can only be used in short, powerful bursts, when should I use it?

Strong minds will deploy willpower as a strategy to overcome a particular obstacle so that other personal strengths can come along later and sustain the victory made with the assault of willpower. I breached a boundary the day I jumped off the diving board. Not only did I pass the test and become an FBI Agent, I was empowered to overcome my fear of water—a few years later I did a 100-foot wall dive in the Grand Cayman, and a few years after that, I learned how to swim ... maybe not the chronological order that others may have preferred but I got there in the end!

My willpower got stronger when I dismissed the doubts I had about abilities, and instead, focused my energies on activities that would develop my strengths. Focusing attention is important for willpower because when there is a need to control the mind, there is less energy available to us for other parts of the body. This is why my other senses were dulled while I was on the diving board.

THINKING ABOUT WILLPOWER

Points to Ponder: Willpower is short bursts of energy to break through a barrier.

Inspiration: *"The will to win is not nearly as important as the will to prepare to win."* —Bobby Knight

Reflection Question: How can willpower make a difference in the way you approach a fierce obstacle?

FLEXIBILITY

"For I know the plans I have for you," says the Lord. "They are plans for good and not disaster, to give you a future and a hope."
— JEREMIAH 29:11 (NEW LIVING TRANSLATION)

Even after graduating from the FBI Academy, all agents must qualify with their weapons four times a year.

Once a year, during these quarterly firearms qualifications, our FBI firearms instructors would give us special guns that shot red paint balls and send us out to discover how much control we had over our physical and mental reflexes. Instead of shooting at targets, we practiced knock-and-announce arrest scenarios where agents were instructed to enter a house and make a series of arrests.

Firearms instructors broke us into groups of five. We took turns being the arrest suspects or the FBI agents making the arrest. Each group had different colored guns.

The suspects were armed and dangerous. They were hiding either inside the house or in the surrounding area. The houses were built as open-air rooms with no roof so catwalks could be constructed above. This is where the firearms instructors observed the arrests, along with the remaining groups of agents waiting until it was their turn.

Nothing goes unnoticed in a paint gun shootout. Every mistake is splattered

187

somewhere—the paint bullets can leave
bruises and stick to hair for days.

No one can hide from the results—mistakes are plastered over every body part. Of more importance, however, were the red splotches that indicated one of our team members had been shot or killed.

We put on goggles and Kevlar helmets; our instructors gave us the arrest scenario and then watched our every decision and the movements required to carry out our decision. We entered houses with trap doors and blind corners, with no obvious plan or path to follow, so had to improvise and adapt to our circumstances as we moved along.

Our goal was to get from one position to another without getting shot and not shooting an innocent bystander. Some of the firearms instructors would walk around inside the house with faces of babies stuck on their chest to indicate an innocent. Split second decisions were made—was this person a friend or a threat? Fellow teammates had guns the same color while the bad guys had guns another color, so blindly shooting or arresting everyone who had a gun was not an option.

When you're in the thick of a paint ball action, all you think about is surviving. You don't want to scrub paint off your clothes when you get home or feel the sting of a paint ball hitting your neck.

In this type of defensive tactics stress course with paint ball guns, every movement called for a re-evaluation of strength, location, and strategy. We never took our eye off the goal of arresting the bad guy, but remained flexible in our approach by constantly re-evaluating our surroundings. We reassessed our strengths in light of changing environments, without becoming complacent or content. Finally, we looked at ways to reinvent ourselves to fit new circumstances instead of relying on old tactics. What worked last time may, or may not, work again this time.

Firearms training with paint ball guns taught me many lessons I later applied to business and life. In a hostile and unpredictable environment, it is important to stay in the moment. There is no time for trying to remember business school formats or emergency preparedness plans. This may sound easy, but it requires determination to keep priorities straight. Being flexible as you carry out your goals is essential in developing a strong mind.

WHAT TO DO WHEN PLANS FAIL

Not every master plan is genius.

Arrest scenarios are notorious for not going according to plan. This happened to me when I made my first arrest in Scottsdale, Arizona. The man under surveillance was a suspect in an extortion case and considered armed and dangerous. I was a rookie, so my training agent took me along with several other seasoned FBI agents as we met outside the suspect's house at sunrise and waited until he got into his car and started moving.

The case agent had a tip from an informant that the man under surveillance was going to meet other people later that morning who had helped plan the extortion. By mid-afternoon, however, he still hadn't met up with anyone, so the agent in charge of the case decided to make a car arrest. The plan was to surround his car with unmarked FBI vehicles. The SWAT trained agents wearing bulletproof vests would jump out, pull the man out of the car, spread-eagle him on the street, place him in handcuffs, and do a pat-down search to find his gun.

If we waited until he returned home, he might have access to guns hidden in the house. And we didn't know who else might be residing there with him.

Unfortunately, the man under surveillance chose the busy street of Scottsdale Road for his return route. The FBI cars traveled in a convoy in hopes of completely surrounding him at a red light. One by one, the FBI cars were cut off due to the high traffic volume. I was riding shotgun in the car that ultimately pulled up next to him at a red light.

In that split second, I knew I had to be the one to step out of the car and make the arrest. We risked losing him in traffic if we waited much longer. It was my first arrest and I was scared. I leaned into my strengths—he was a big man and I knew I could not manhandle him out of the car. I needed to take him by surprise and be prepared to use my gun if he made any furtive movements or resisted arrest.

I chose not to wear my FBI raid jacket as I stepped out of the car because I didn't want to alert the man of my identity. I don't look like a typical FBI agent and was wearing a long sweater that concealed my gun. The man noticed me and was surprised when I smiled, leaned over, and politely tapped on his window. He rolled down his window and smiled back. I pulled out my gun, advised him he was under arrest, and told him to put his hands up.

His jaw dropped and his foot slipped off the clutch. The car jolted into the intersection and stalled. Traffic around us stopped and I heard a crash as two cars collided in the distance. He sat in the car with his hands held high as I reached over to open the door and ordered him to get out.

By this time, other agents had arrived on the scene and hand-cuffed him. When we searched the car, we found a loaded weapon under the driver's seat.

Even though my team's plans had changed, simply because of traffic patterns, the key to our successfully and peaceably arresting him was a determination to see the situation through to the end, no matter the change in circumstances. Determination allowed me to keep my goal in mind while being flexible enough to adapt to changes in my environment.

THINKING ABOUT FLEXIBILITY

Point to Ponder: It's OK to make plans; just make them in pencil.

Inspiration: *"Running water never goes stale."* —Bruce Lee

Reflection Question: When have you demonstrated the greatest flexibility?

PERSISTENCE

"The majority of people meet with failure because of their lack of persistence in creating new plans to take the place of those which fail."

—NAPOLEAN HILL

The winters in Wyoming are long and harsh.

The ranch where I grew up was near Laramie Peak and a great deal of my life revolved around stacking bales of hay in the warm months so we could load it onto a pickup truck in the cold and snowy months to feed our cattle. I never thought much about building upper body strength during those years—I just wanted to get the job done so I could get on with the more interesting things in life that consumes the mind of a teenager.

My life changed dramatically when I entered the FBI Academy at Quantico. The focus was on building upper body strength, again—only this time, instead of stacking bales of hay it was the pushups that were required to graduate from the Academy. I've talked about my difficulties in building upper body strength in earlier chapters. While I lacked confidence in my abilities, I also knew I had to be persistent in my efforts to achieve my goals.

My coach told me to "kiss the ground I walked on" if I expected him to "count" my every pushup. Although I had grown up throwing around 50 pound bales of hay, I had a difficult time mustering the strength to do a pushup that counted in the eyes of my coach.

I questioned how gutting out the perfect push-up was going to make me a better investigator or make it easier to find foreign spies. But there was no choice: every day at the FBI Academy involved some kind of physical activity. Because I wasn't as physically fit as the other new agents, I put in extra training for the FIT test. As a new agent's class, we boxed each other, engaged in arrest scenarios, and ran around the basketball court holding 5 lb. medicine balls. I was tired, depressed, and under pressure, but I knew that if I gave up, I'd regret it the rest of my life.

I had to come to terms with certain facts about myself. I had always perceived myself as a physically strong ranch girl who could ride a horse and work cattle as well as any rancher. I had been talented at saddling horses, cutting bulls from herds of cattle, and working with livestock. I entered the FBI Academy quite confident in my physical abilities. On the very first day, I was forced to see myself in a different light, and it was up to me to decide how to move forward with this new information.

"Blocks usually turn into stepping stones."
—LOLLY DASKAL[12]

My environment had drastically changed. The people who were now my colleagues represented the cream of the crop. I was not in the same category of athletes as many of the other new agents but that did not matter. I had to look hard and deep to find qualities in which I excelled, but I persevered and found them—I was a great shot and possessed an analytical mind that helped me connect the moving parts in many of our training interviews.

I would not give up. I would learn to survive in this new environment in which I found myself.

It's impossible to be an excellent performer without persistence. Giving up is easy. Anyone can do that. When you do, you surrender.

> Persistence is continuing to move ahead even when life hasn't dealt you a perfect hand. It is the deliberate action of doing something again and again until you get it right. And then maybe doing it again after that, too. If you can dig deep and find the discipline to persist, you can harness a power that has unlimited potential.

Nothing can take the place of persistence. Talent will not. Nothing is more common than unsuccessful people with talent. Genius cannot make you successful; unrewarded genius is almost a proverb. Persistence and determination alone will keep you moving ahead to achieve your goal.

Often, it is not the brilliance of your achievement that impresses others; it is your ability to persist, against the odds, in meeting your goal.

KEEP YOUR EYE ON THE GOAL

You must know where you want to go in life, not merely be inclined toward something or thinking about it. This is important because unless you know your goal, you cannot identify the immediate next steps that are needed to move forward with purpose.

My goal when I was in college was not just to graduate with a Bachelor's degree in Business. My goal was to find a good career that would provide me with opportunities to move beyond the confines of my environment in Wyoming. I knew that if I didn't leave during my college years, I never would.

I used strategy and remained persistent in achieving each step. The steps were small; I first transferred from the University of Wyoming to Northern Arizona University, which was approximately the size of the UW so I wouldn't feel as though I was in over my head. Once I got adjusted, I then transferred to Arizona State University. After graduating, my first job was working as a department manager at a large national retail chain store based in Phoenix called Diamonds. I was moving ahead in my career.

My focus never left my ultimate goal, but I persisted over several years and used different strategies to move closer to it. Once I had achieved my goal, I found myself in an environment that presented far more opportunities than I could have found if I had never left Wyoming.

As I mentioned in an earlier chapter, the FBI recruited me while I was completing graduate studies in Organizational Communication at Arizona State University. As a child, I had been drawn to the need of protecting animals from cruelty; as an adult, I was lured by the opportunity offered by the FBI to do something even bigger with my life—protecting the rights of people victimized by others.

Once I set my eyes on my goal of becoming an FBI agent, I used the strategy of small steps. I worked hard studying and reading so I would pass the written and oral tests, which I did with flying colors. Six months after I sent in my application to be considered for a position as an FBI agent, I received my letter of acceptance. I had rated twelfth in a pool of twenty-five thousand applicants.

Life at the FBI Academy, however, presented a different set of challenges. There were several times when I felt like quitting. My level of motivation was inconsistent; sometimes it was there and at other times it was not. But my actions were more important—persistence kept me moving forward even when I wasn't highly motivated to do so. In the process, the results began to accumulate. The more I worked on my pushups, the more progress I began to see. And then I became more motivated to continue my workouts.

PERSISTENCE IS NOT STUBBORNESS

I straightened my back at the FBI Academy and dug deeper.

I'd taken the final FIT test and missed qualifying—by one point. The physical test consisted of pushups, pull-ups, sit-ups, short sprints, and a two-mile run—in that order. I failed to perform the minimum number of pushups and knew I failed the test in less than ten minutes after I started. I wanted to drop out of the rest of the test at that point—I mean, what was the point of finishing it? My coach would not let me. He said, "No agent ever quits at anything they start—ever."

The next few days would determine my future. One of my FBI counselors, a kind gentleman named John Finnegan, saw me sitting alone on a bench in front of the FBI Academy shortly after the final FIT test. I faced the real possibility of being washed out of the program. He sat down beside me and told me that I would have been sent home earlier that day if my FBI counselors had not been impressed by my determination, willpower, and perseverance. Because of these qualities, they were prepared to work with me and give me another opportunity to pass the FIT test.

Each new agent's class had two experienced agents from field offices assigned to the Academy as counselors. John was one of those counselors. In addition, each class was assigned five physical fitness coaches to help us make it through the FIT test. Two weeks later, I took the additional FIT alone, except for my FBI counselors and a couple of the physical fitness coaches. No one from my new agents class was invited. I got up at 6:00AM that morning to begin the test at 6:30AM. I was to join the rest of my class for our morning lecture on search and seizure.

What went through my mind? Throwing bales of hay when I was a teenager, digging fence pole holes, running cattle and beating back horned bulls that were bigger and meaner than I. I was not a prissy, but it wasn't the others I needed to convince, it was myself.

I saw myself as different; others saw me as unique. In the early years of my life, I wasn't so certain that unique was better, or stronger. I just wanted to be like my classmates. My conversation with John Finnegan helped me understand how others viewed my difference as both beautiful and strong. I had spent too much energy trying to conform to what others thought of me. I had constructed my own wall of self-limiting beliefs. Knowing that John believed that I had what it took to be an FBI agent, I passed the FIT test on that chilly early morning.

I joined my other new agents in the lecture hall. They all looked pensive because everyone knew that if I didn't pass this FIT test, I would be gone by the end of the day. No one said a word, but the coaches let it slip that I had made enough points to graduate from the Academy. Before this announcement, the tension had been so thick that the air was hard to breathe. It lessened a little that day when we knew the entire class would be graduating—together.

HOW TO GET WHAT YOU REALLY WANT

In the summer of 1855, sixteen-year-old John D. Rockefeller needed a job.

He had just completed a three-month course in bookkeeping, and he made a list of the companies in his hometown of Cleveland that might need a bookkeeper's assistant. Cleveland was booming with business, but no one was willing to take a chance on someone so young and inexperienced. For weeks, Rockefeller spent six days a week walking hot streets in his suit and tie, trying to find work. He was rejected from every business on his list.

Rockefeller responded to this potentially crushing setback by simply starting over, requesting interviews from the same firms that had denied him days earlier. Eventually, an executive in a produce shipping company rewarded Rockefeller's persistence and hired the boy who would become the richest and most powerful businessman in the world.

BE PERSISTENT

Pushups taught me a great deal about persistence.

Many of our most important goals require persistence if we want to achieve them. I learned that there are ways to increase persistence—and here are some of the techniques that helped me:

Face my problems head on. My image of myself didn't reflect reality because when I looked in the mirror, I saw an athlete. Taking a long, hard look at my assets and liabilities was an important first step. At the same time, it was just as important that I not judge myself as unfit or unqualified because I had encountered a weak spot.

Physical fitness was an area of weakness and I needed to face it. I had very little definition in my biceps, and my muscular legs were better suited to slow, long distance than a short and fast two-mile run. I had to muster my way through if I planned to graduate from the Academy. I was not going to let my problem define me, but it wasn't going to go away unless I did something about it.

I needed to be honest about what I wanted to achieve, who I wanted to become, and identify the obstacles that were preventing me from achieving my goals. At one level, I faced physical limitations, but persistence at physical training would allow me to overcome my obstacles. It would take hard work and determination. I had to be honest in every aspect of my life because I know that I am the one person who always has my best interests at heart.

Define My Goal as Behavior. I needed to perform thirty-five pushups to qualify in the FIT test. Men and women performed the same type of pushups. Knowing this, I set my goal on forty-five pushups. By now, the Academy had taught me that the minimum is never acceptable. If we were told to run ten laps, we ran eleven. If told to do forty sit-ups, we did forty-one. From day one, our unofficial motto was always, "More than the minimum required."

Take Small Steps. I started with a realistic number in my head—five pushups to start. And then worked my way up.

Organize My Day. This was crucial for me because I'm a morning person. If I need to accomplish important things, they need to be done early.

Once I set my goal, it became a priority. This is often where weak wills meet rubber roads. Wishing for something to happen won't make it happen. I reorganized my day so I had time to make my goal a reality. I set my alarm clock for 6:00AM every morning and did forty-five pushups. Instead, of joining the others for lunch, I grabbed an apple and would run or workout in the Academy's gym.

Remember the Reasons I Wanted to Reach My Goal. When I felt down or lacked motivation, I always remembered why I was there and what I wanted my future to look like.

When I felt my determination begin to waver, I would remember the reason I wanted to accomplish my goal.

Watch for Excuses. Working out with one of my fellow new agents helped keep me accountable. He was patient and gave me pointers on ways I could improve my sit-ups, two mile run, and pushups. I was actually quite good at pull-ups and didn't need to work on that one area. Working out with my colleague prevented me from making excuses or not go to the next step in my workout program.

PERSISTENCE IS ONE STEP AT A TIME

Persistence was getting myself to do something I didn't want to do. I didn't give myself permission to come up with an excuse to avoid working toward my goal. Getting into a routine was very important. There were times when I felt as though I'd made no progress, but I would not give in. The steps toward building my strong mind culminated in developing the habit of doing what I needed to do to reach my goal.

Every day I kept at it, making a little progress at a time. The Academy lasted four months and I worked on my physical fitness requirements every day. In retrospect, I have to say that my lesson in pushups was one of the most valuable I learned in my training: persistence is the key to unlocking life's obstacles. Instead of seeing them as threats, they are simply challenges to be met.

THINKING ABOUT PERSISTENCE

Point to Ponder: Persistence is not stubbornness.

Inspiration: *"That which we persist in doing becomes easier— not because the nature of the task has changed, but our ability to do it has changed."* —Ralph Waldo Emerson

Reflection Question: How has persistence helped you achieve an important goal in your life?

DETERMINATION TACTICS

WILLPOWER

If you fill your mind with the right attitude, grit and determination can be learned. Here are a few pointers to keep your mind strong:

Formulate in your mind a mental picture of yourself succeeding. Never allow this picture to fade. Do not think of yourself as failing because the mind will try to complete what is pictured there.

Cancel negative thoughts with a positive one. When you begin to doubt whether you can continue to move toward your goal, deliberately do a "voice over" to cancel it out. Say it out loud or write it down to etch it more firmly in your mind.

Minimize obstacles in your mind. Do not allow them to build up and become giants. You must confront the difficulties, but see them for what they truly are. Don't allow fear to blow them out of proportion.

Find a mantra you can repeat during the day. The words need to be dynamic and provide you with motivation to keep moving forward. It can be a poem, song, or scripture. For example, I keep the words of the Apostle Paul close: *"I've got my eye on the goal, where God is beckoning us onward ... I'm off and running, and I'm not turning back."* Philippians 3:13-14 *The Message*

Get a coach. It's very difficult to see yourself clearly and a coach—whether a physical fitness or career coach—is someone who can help point out why you do what you do. They will be able to pinpoint the times when you lack the grit to persevere in reaching your goal.

Make a realistic estimate of your own ability. Don't be egotistical. Be realistic about your strengths and weaknesses. Now, raise your expectation of performance by 10%. Once you've reached the higher performance, raise it again by another 10%. The bottom line: believe in yourself.

FLEXIBILITY

These are some ways to let go of plans and be more flexible:

Stop the Need to Be in Control. No matter who we are or what we do, we can't always see the big picture. Disruptions in our plans are seen only as inconveniences or obstacles. We assume we always know what is best and that God will honor the blueprints we have designed for our life. Man plans; God laughs. Rest in the knowledge that there is a bigger plan that neither you nor I are aware of.

1. What plan for your life failed to go as expected?

2. How did you react?

3. How did you cope?

4. Would you handle your response differently now?

5. How do you attempt to control your environment?

6. What are the ways you train your ability to control your reaction to your environment?

Embrace the Uncomfortable. When we make plans for ourselves, we steer away from the unpleasant. That's why we make plans to begin with. Few of us would choose the path with the biggest bumps and roadblocks. However, it's the unexpected curveballs that provide us the biggest area of growth and self-awareness. We cannot explore or understand the unknown unless we get close enough to examine it. The unknown is uncomfortable because we can't plan for it.

1. Name an unpleasant experience on your current path.

2. What have you learned from it?

3. How would you have learned the same lesson if you hadn't experienced it?

4. How did the experience lead to greater self-awareness?

Move Out of the Past. We draw up plans based on what we have seen, experienced, or imagine to be true. Too often, however, perception does not reflect reality. Even if our past experiences are correct, circumstances change. We find deception and volatility in advertising, investments, and politics. What worked in the past may not work in the future.

1. What past pattern of thinking has limited you in reaching your potential?

2. What unplanned circumstance opened up new possibilities for you?

3. How has an unexpected event created a better version of you?

4. Can you pinpoint an instance when you did not move ahead because of a self-limiting belief?

Avoid Complacency. Many times we make plans because we're stuck in a rut and we don't know what else to do. We rely on a plan and use it as an excuse for not living our life as the adventure we should be living. If we're in a job that is unfulfilling, why aren't we doing something about it? Does our plan have something to do with it? If it does, chuck the plan.

1. How have you used your plans as an excuse for being stuck?

2. When has it been harder to chuck your plan or make a new one rather than stay put?

3. When making plans, have you done something crazy and unpredictable?

4. If you did do something crazy and unpredictable, what would it be?

5. What does your dream for your life look like?

PERSISTENCE

These are ways you can become more persistent:

Name an important goal. Develop a strategy to achieve it.

Accept that failure happens. Successful people in life have all failed. The difference between them and people who live in fear of failure is that they learn from it and use it spur on their next attempt.

Ask yourself: What is my attitude toward failure? Am I avoiding it by never persisting at anything? Am I using fear

---

of failure to avoid being persistent in my current goals and actions?

Examine the reasons that might be leading to failure. You may need to tweak your approach if you continue to hit road bumps.

Stop and assess the things you're doing to reach your goals. Sometimes it's not the goal, it's the fine details that haven't been clarified or properly tailored to reach the goal.

If you are determined, you can accomplish anything. There will be failures along the way, but they will only be setbacks. You may need to change your plans and strategies to overcome certain roadblocks, but they will help you clarify your destination. The failures and change of plans may mean your goal looks different from what you first envisioned, but with determination you will keep moving forward. Without determination, you're doomed to frustration and disappointment. As you move toward your goal, the next characteristic of a strong mind you will need is resilience.

CHAPTER 6

RESILIENCE

"Character cannot be developed in ease and quiet. Only through experience of trial and suffering can the soul be strengthened, vision cleared, ambition inspired, and success achieved."

—HELEN KELLER

I was viewed as a curiosity more than anything else.

In the early 1980's there weren't many female FBI agents, and when I walked into my new field office, everyone was polite but distant. I wore a suit and low-heeled shoes—despite what is shown in movies and TV shows, nothing looks more ridiculous than a woman trying to be taken seriously as she totters around trying to balance the weight of a gun on her hip while wearing high heels.

I was the only woman on the squad. My supervisor called me "Junior Boots," the official title taken on by the newest agent on the squad, male or female. I was assigned the lowest priority cases, and since I had the least experience, that made sense. Working hard and keeping my nose to the grindstone, I pretended not to notice when other squad members grabbed their jackets and headed out the door for lunch without inviting me. Often, I would stay at my desk and work through the lunch hour.

I also pretended not to notice when everyone else on the squad made arrangements to meet for breakfast before heading out to firearms training every couple of months, also without inviting me. That same day, at firearms, the squad would shoot together and go out to lunch together—again, without inviting me.

Occasionally, one of the guys would break rank and stop to chat. Those gestures were appreciated, but they came rarely. I didn't expect special treatment because I was a woman, but I did expect to be treated fairly. In essence, I wanted to be one of the guys.

The other agents came back into the office after an interview and talked amongst themselves about what they had learned and how they planned to utilize the information in their cases. They put together undercover proposals for the undercover review board and speculated on how they intended to utilize their undercover agent (UCA) to get next to a hostile intelligence officer.

Only senior agents were considered experienced enough to be investigating the activities of an intelligence officer.

It soon became evident, however, that I would never get the opportunity as long as I was assigned the cases no one else on the squad wanted. If I wanted to work against a foreign spy, I'd need to go out and find one myself.

Persistent, I continued to look for ways to make this happen. As much as the rest of the squad postured and pontificated about their big cases, not one of them was actually working as an undercover agent. Although they put in effort and toiled, their approach to hostile intelligence officers looked tired and transparent. In summary, they needed fresh tactics.

The agents that I approached with different ideas listened, but no one took me seriously. I didn't know if it was my inexperience or because they were uncomfortable with my suggestions. My supervisor told me that I needed to put something down on paper before he'd consider it. When I did, he turned my idea over to one of the senior agents and I never heard anything about it again.

The answer finally dawned on me—I would start my own undercover operation! Normally, the case agent writes an undercover proposal that is specifically directed at the foreign spy that is assigned to them. Once it's approved, an agent who has attended Undercover In-Service training and been vetted by the Behavioral Science Unit is identified and placed in the role. Since I didn't have a hostile intelligence officer assigned to me, I spent several weeks writing an undercover proposal where I would assume the role of the UCA. It was a back-to-front approach, but it was worth a try. I was going nowhere if I didn't do something.

The proposal was crafted to play on my personal strengths, thus adding authenticity to my undercover identity. My plan was to ingratiate myself into think tank communities to uncover spies sent to the U.S. to steal military, political, and economic information. It was a long shot, and different from traditional undercover operations because it cast a wide net instead of targeting one specific individual of interest, but my youth gave me credibility as a student interested in international public relations. This was a trump card I had to play against my older male squad mates—they looked, acted, and talked like seasoned FBI agents. I did not.

FBI Headquarters loved the proposal. They recognized the need to be proactive and not rely on the tired approaches that had been used for years. I needed to find a case agent to oversee the net we were throwing out so I approached one of my squad mates. He agreed, and we've been good friends ever since. The lower priority cases were assigned to another male agent on the squad. That was the last time in my career I waited for the good assignments to come to me. Instead, I just went after them.

This was not the first time I'd needed persistence to move forward in life …

THE FEEL OF ISOLATION

I attended a private school until I turned thirteen. We lived too far from the nearest town to be bused to a public school. Miles of dirt roads isolated our little schoolhouse on the ranch, so neither my brother nor I had friends or many social graces.

We rarely associated with the few other kids who also lived on remote ranches in Albany County. Several of them chose to obtain their high school diploma through correspondence rather than go to a public school. And a few who did try to make the transition to a public school failed when they lost their resolve, gave up, and returned to the ranch.

After I finished seventh grade, our family moved to my Grandfather's ranch that was only half an hour from a small rural community named Wheatland. Attending public school after spending the first seven years in a one-room country schoolhouse with two students was a painful transition. I tried hard to fit in with the other students, but I was little more than a hillbilly in the eyes of the others. I looked and dressed differently; clothes that work in a small schoolhouse in the middle of nowhere are not appropriate for an anxious fashion-conscious teenager.

The other students ignored me, but this only strengthened my resolve and forced me to become creative and self-reliant. I became more determined with every setback and sought out other students in the school who were also ignored or marginalized. They became my few friends, and while the bond was not strong, I began to learn the socialization skills that had been absent from my one-room schoolhouse, but I was years behind my peers in understanding the social issues of my community and world.

Adding to my isolation, I couldn't stay after school for extracurricular activities or sports because I had chores and responsibilities waiting for me back at the ranch. I had no car until I was in college, so my parents had to spend an hour driving me to and from town if I wanted to participate in activities with kids my own age. In those days, parents had a life of their own and didn't find running around as a chauffeur for their kids as glamorous as parents apparently seem to do these days.

I needed to adapt to my new circumstances as a teenager going to a public school, and because of my resilience, I was able to overcome obstacles in my path. But I've come to believe there is more to resilience. Although I was rough on the outside as a newcomer to my school, I clung to the values I had developed in my childhood. Somewhere deep down, I started embracing the person that my experiences created me to be. I survived in my new environment because I leaned into the core character strengths I learned while facing down a fighting bull when I was ten years old, running over a coiled rattlesnake while riding my bicycle, and saddling a nasty tempered pony named Socks.

I developed my own strategy for coping: I tried to get noticed for my achievements. I entered and re-entered every contest and competition for which I qualified—anything that would build my confidence and gain me respect among my classmates. Year after year I entered school speech tournaments, art shows, and 4-H demonstrations. Year after year, I failed to win anything. Perseverance, determination, and resilience prodded me forward as I fought to distinguish myself in some way. I did not give up.

The fact that I did not fit in with most of the others sometimes got me down, but I knew I needed to keep a positive attitude or I'd disappear into despair before my life had even started.

These years of adversity lasted until my senior year when I finally won something. It was a speech tournament, and once momentum started, I found myself being honored with bigger things as well. That first moment of achievement showed me how a strong mind can help overcome adversity.

TOUGH STUFF

We've all had to navigate through challenging times toward a better future. Those of us who are resilient know how to bounce back from adversity. The human spirit is surprisingly resilient. Resilience is the faith that you will land on your feet. Part of it comes from your upbringing and environment. It is also something you can learn to cultivate and practice to prepare for the challenges that lie ahead.

To deepen our understanding of resilience, we will look at 3 components: adversity, failure, and a positive attitude.

THINKING ABOUT RESILIENCE

Point to Ponder: The human spirit is woven from tough and resilient fabric.

Inspiration: *"Inside of a ring or out, ain't nothing wrong with going down. It's staying down that's wrong."*—Mohammed Ali

Reflection Question: What does it mean to you to be resilient? How have you survived tough times?

ADVERSITY

"When written in Chinese, the word "crisis" is composed of two characters—one represents danger and the other represents opportunity."
—JOHN F. KENNEDY

Rattlesnakes, not drugs, were the biggest threat I faced while growing up on our Wyoming ranch.

I wore lace-up work boots everywhere to protect myself from being bitten by a rattler while walking through sagebrush and over rocks. Not exactly a stunning fashion accessory, but getting a brand new pair that had thick soles and smelled of leather was a favorite Christmas present every year.

Since we lived a couple of hours from the nearest hospital, the poisonous venom from a rattlesnake bite could kill us before we found help. My brother and I learned how to cut the bite marks with a knife and extract the poison. Rattlesnakes blend into sagebrush and rocks and it was difficult to see them unless we were constantly diligent. My parents drilled this into my thinking from when I was a toddler—rattlesnakes were my biggest predator growing up.

At eleven years of age, I rode my bike on a cow trail east of our ranch house. Hundreds of cow hooves moving to meadows along the North Laramie River had worn a deep rut into the earth. The narrow path exposed sharp rocks and tufts of tough grass so it was a bumpy ride, but I had thick tires and never had a blowout.

216

It was easy to pick up speed as I followed the cow path downhill alongside the river. The water was moving fast and I played a game of racing a three-foot long stick that I'd thrown in when I left the house. I kept my focus on avoiding the sharper rocks on the path but I sped along at a good clip. Too fast, it seems, to notice a coiled rattlesnake on the other side of a rock that I was about to run over—until the snake struck out at full length.

My bike flipped, and as I landed, I felt dozens of pricks all over my arms and hands. My mind raced with fear because I thought the rattlesnake had repeatedly bitten me. I did not have a penknife with me. At eleven, I prepared myself to die of snake poisoning.

Right about the time I was mourning the loss of what could have been a spectacular life, I noticed that I had landed in a pile of cactus. The wreck of my bike told me the rest of the story— the snake had struck the spokes of the front wheel and was now struggling to get out of the broken and bent spoke wires.

> **My first instinct was to run home to safety, but my parents had taught me that nothing would be accomplished by running away from adversity.**

Living on a remote ranch meant that I had to be ready to face a crisis on my own because there would not be anyone else around to fight my battle for me. The first thing I did was to find a good sized rock and make sure that particular rattlesnake would never terrorize my cow lane, or any other, again.

I picked out the cactus needles, one by one. Then I loaded the bike on my shoulders and carried the sorry mess home.

PAST ADVERSITY PREDICTS FUTURE SUCCESS

Some things fall apart in life so that better things can fall together.

New research[13] suggests that resilience to adversity in life may be linked to how often we face it. The number of blows a person has taken may affect their mental toughness more than any other factor.

The study showed that the frequency of adversities faced by an individual in the past assists them in developing resilience to adversities in the future.

Some participants in the study had lived a charmed life and had faced little or no adversity in their lives. The researchers found that their sense of wellbeing was about the same as those who had suffered several memorable blows in life. The participants who scored the highest in wellbeing were those reporting two to six stressful events. Those who had experienced more than a dozen stressful events found it difficult to cope.

In short, the findings suggest that a strong mind is something like physical strength: it cannot develop without exercise and it breaks down when overworked.

Furthermore, a person with a strong mind can predict the way they will respond to adversity.

Here are 5 things I'm glad I learned about developing resilience and overcoming adversity:

Confront the negative. I learned a great deal from my mistakes and failures when I wasn't too busy denying them. After continuing to ask myself the same questions for months, or years, I realized I was stuck. I knew the answers—I just didn't like them. It took courage to admit things needed to change, and a lot more courage for me to accept responsibility for actually changing them. The most difficult step was the first one. Once I had momentum started, positive changes began to build on each other.

Face adversity, don't avoid it. The study cited above reflects how easy it is to take good luck for granted. If I was not prepared for adversity when it came, I would have no tools with which to fight back. Not getting what I wanted forced me to identify my core character strengths and personal values.

Expect the deepest pain to empower you to your full potential. It's not a pleasant thought, but very often it is the stressful choices that end up being the most worthwhile. Without pain, there would be no change. I vowed to learn all I could from my pain every time I faced adversity so I would be better prepared to learn from it in the future.

Work outside your comfort zone. I learned to accept a new responsibility or challenge even if I didn't think I was ready for it. It was OK to acknowledge that I needed additional information, skill, or experience—no one is 100% ready when an opportunity arises. Most opportunities in life forced me to grow, both emotionally and intellectually. They forced me out of my comfort zone. If I wanted to build resilience and overcome adversity, I would need to embrace moments of uncertainty even though I didn't feel 100% ready for them.

Embrace the lesson. Everything happens for a reason. I have the attitude that things go wrong so I can learn to appreciate things when they go right. I have learned to embrace the lesson each opportunity has to teach me so I can recognize the circumstances surrounding those lessons the next time they show up.

THINKING ABOUT ADVERSITY

Point to Ponder: Adversity allows you to become acquainted with yourself.

Inspiration: *"Adversity reveals genius; prosperity conceals it."*—Horace

Reflection Question: How has adversity shaped you into a better person today?

FAILURE

"Success is the ability to go from one failure to another with no loss of enthusiasm."

—WINSTON CHURCHILL

About halfway through the FBI Academy I learned that climbing a twenty-foot rope was a physical requirement for new agents. The problem was that everyone else in my class could do it—except me.

Day after day, time and time again, I'd get about one third of the way up and just couldn't pull myself up any farther. It was a bare rope with no knots, and since everyone else had climbed ropes before, there was no instruction on how to do it. Like swimming, the coaches assumed everyone knew how.

I was fatigued, and at some point, avoiding rope burn became as much of a goal as climbing because I needed to get down safely. It was humiliating to know that I needed to prepare for failure on each climb as well as prepare for eventual success.

But over time I realized that the same skills I needed to prepare for failure would also be needed if I succeeded because I still had to get back *down* the rope.

Trust me when I say that retreating day after day was harder than moving ahead. I needed to think long term as well as short term. On one occasion I thought I might make it to the top if

I really pushed, but how would I get down—with dignity and without injury?

Success meant climbing the rope. So I kept at it. Athletes get psyched up before games and competition because the real battle lines are drawn in the mind. I knew if I began to doubt whether or not I'd ever be able to climb the rope, I wouldn't. I needed to keep my mind strong by optimism and positive thinking.

Once my classmates realized I had never climbed a rope, they began giving me instructions on how to wrap the rope around my leg and use my leg muscles to pull myself up, instead of relying entirely on upper body strength. With their help, I managed to climb the rope and reach the top.

HOW TO FAIL BETTER

Samuel Becket asked a brilliant question: *"How can we fail better?"*

The difference between successful people and those who are not is a matter of how often they try. Successful people fail just as often, perhaps more so because they keep picking themselves up again and again. They keep trying new things until at last they find something that works. They push past the negative attitudes and depression that comes with failure.

Why are some people more resilient? Why is it that the same set of circumstances that drives one person deeper into the mud makes another stronger? Failure is one of life's most common traumas, yet people's responses to it vary widely. Some bounce back after a brief period of malaise; others continue to descent into depression and a fear of the future.

Thomas Edison threw himself into his work. While he was trying to invent the light bulb, he failed over 10,000 times. He worked long hours, but his persistence and resilience led to the creation of the incandescent light bulb. Edison did not look at these 10,000 attempts as failures; rather, he saw them as 10,000 lessons about how not to make a light bulb.

I found that overcoming failure is as much about being motivated as it is about having the right talent. I eventually did climb the rope and get back down without burn marks by getting out every day and taking incremental steps toward attaining my goal.

FAILURE DOESN'T MEAN IT'S OVER

Failure provides an opportunity to make a decision and then take action.

Failure forces you to think about what is most important to you. Colonel Sanders, the founder of Kentucky Fried Chicken, is an excellent example of someone who took action to make life better, even when those actions met with failure time and time again.

In the 1930's, Harland Sanders used his cooking skills to provide meals for travelers who stopped at his service station in Kentucky. His specialty was fried chicken seasoned with his original blend of eleven herbs and spices. In 1935, he was made an honorary Kentucky Colonel because of his acclaimed cooking skills.

At the age of 65, Colonel Sanders received his first social security check for $105. As he looked back over his life, it seemed a series of failure that brought him to an impoverished old age. He was disappointed, but instead of blaming the government or society, he began to think about how he could try to change the remainder of his life so that it would both have more meaning and produce an income that he could comfortably live on.

He had a chicken recipe that everyone seemed to love and thought that he might be able to sell it to restaurants and make enough money to pay his rent. Then he began to think that if he could show the restaurants how to cook the chicken properly, they would make even more sales. If they made more money, maybe they'd give him a percentage of the sales.

When Colonel Sanders went knocking on doors in his trademark white suit, he was no longer just selling a recipe; he was selling a formula that would increase their sales. And he wanted a percentage of those sales! Most people laughed in his face, but Colonel Sanders did not give up. Instead of feeling bad about his rejection, he used what he had learned from the rejection so he could tell his story more effectively and get better results at the next restaurant.

He spent two years driving across America in his old car, sleeping in the back seat in his rumpled white suit, and getting up each morning to share his idea with someone new. He cooked batches of chicken from restaurant to restaurant and often, the only food he had were the samples he was preparing for perspective buyers. He experienced failure and was rejected 1,009 times.

Eventually, he struck a deal that paid him a nickel for every chicken a restaurant sold. The chicken became so successful that Colonel Sanders was able to franchise Kentucky Fried Chicken.

People with resilient minds do not stop when they are rejected or fail. They do not accept no as an answer. They do not let anything stop them from making their goal a reality.

HOW TO FAIL BETTER

Here are some lessons I learned about failure:

Start. I kept putting off climbing the rope, even after I knew I'd need to do it. There is no better way to overcome the fear of failure than to start moving toward the goal. Not starting is the failure.

Stay positive. I needed to find a way to stay positive, even when I felt overwhelmed by my circumstances. My positive thinking helped me consider my goal not just a possibility, but also a probability. I knew that everyone who has achieved greatness has had to overcome obstacles. I thought back to some of the barriers I have overcome in my life by using positive language and spoke in phrases like "I want," "I will," and "I like."

Celebrate and remember my successes. My current successes needed to be celebrated; my past ones needed to be remembered. They were a powerful motivator when I faced failure in the future.

Find a friendly competitor. I found other new agents who were either willing to help me learn to climb the rope or who needed to work on it as well. They brought out the competitive spirit in me. They knew my goals, and my difficulties. They helped hold me accountable.

Visualize. I imagined how events would unfold. I saw myself winning or achieving my goal. I formed a clear mental picture several times a day. It was an effective way for me to get into a positive frame of mind. I also found images that represented my goal and used them as screen savers or posted them in places I'd see them regularly.

Learn from past experiences. I was not afraid to look at my past performances and mistakes as part of the growth process. Just because an endeavor did not end as well as I had hoped it would, it didn't mean I couldn't learn from it. Defeat is only a temporary condition; giving up is what makes it permanent.

"I've missed more than 9000 shots in my career. I've lost almost 300 games. 26 times I've been trusted to take the game winning shot and missed. I've failed over and over and over again in my life. And that is why I succeed."
—MICHAEL JORDAN

Breakdown goals. I used the strategy of small steps and took small bites at a time. Wrapping my leg around the rope correctly, pulling myself up a foot at a time, adding another foot the next day, and sliding back the rope as gracefully as I moved up. One day I was able to touch the top of the knotted rope, pause for a moment, and then slowly ease my way back down—without rope burn on either my hands or my legs. I had done it!

Talk it up. I told people what I was doing to keep the conversation around me animated and supportive. I announced that I was going to achieve my goal by a deadline. It helped hold me accountable to my timeframe.

The real battle between success and failure is played in the mind. Whether you are defeated by your failures, or overcome obstacles, depends upon a strong mind. Thomas Edison believed the human mind was capable of anything, and so do I.

THINKING ABOUT FAILURE

Point to Ponder: Success and failure are both temporary conditions.

Inspiration: *"When you're going through Hell, by all means, keep going."*—Winston Churchill

Reflection Question: How do you visualize success?

POSITIVE ATTITUDE

"If you have a positive attitude and constantly strive to give your best effort, eventually you will overcome your immediate problems and find you are ready for greater challenges."

—PAT RILEY

I learned the importance of keeping a positive attitude while working the undercover case that I mentioned at the beginning of this chapter.

Every so often, a foreign spy comes to the U.S. who is knowledgeable in the area in which they are assigned to collect information. They are usually the most formidable, because they know what they're talking about. Most foreign intelligence officers, however, are given assignments and learn on the job. It's not uncommon for someone with experience in science to be given an assignment to collect political information. These "newbies" are much easier for the FBI to spot, because the questions they ask people they meet in their new field are so elementary. They also tend to lack passion for the subject matter, and don't follow up on topics not directly related to their assignment.

For us, however, they are a godsend when we are working undercover, because the FBI agent can become as much of an expert as the spy—maybe more so with the right backstopping (or false background.) Establishing credibility with the target, in this case the foreign agent, is the first and most important goal of an undercover operation. I talked about Nicholas in an earlier chapter. Once I had established credibility by attending conferences and being perceived as a legitimate member of the group, the relationship I ultimately established with him was personal, and revolved around his changing feelings toward life goals and purpose.

Each case evolves differently. One of my most vexing cases involved a Russian intelligence officer who was a very tall and thin man with a narrow fringe of dark hair atop a small head perched on a long neck. We called him the "Balding Eagle."

The Balding Eagle was interested in collecting political intelligence. He moved around think tanks and universities, where experts are routinely called upon by the Administration to join Washington policymakers in analyzing world events, sometimes to formulate a political response. These experts are given clearances classified SECRET, briefed on international events, then asked for their opinions about American foreign policy on specific issues. Sneaking into this process, or "Keeping a step ahead of the Americans" is a strategic political game played not only by our enemies, but also by many of our allies.

The Balding Eagle was not an expert in U.S. foreign policy, the area to which he was assigned, so I knew he would rely heavily on informants. The information we collected from other intelligence services suggested that he had a strong background in military operations. This produced an opportunity for me as an undercover agent. As part of the undercover operation, the FBI and the U.S. State Department armed me with enough information and insight to convince him that he was talking to a well-connected bureaucrat—someone who was authorized to discuss the intricacies of U.S. foreign policy.

I had arranged for a HUMINT source to introduce me to the Balding Eagle during a lecture series at a think tank. The source and I had arranged earlier that our association would be neither long term or strong—that way, if the Balding Eagle ever suspected me of being an FBI agent, it would not reflect negatively on the source. My backstopping came from the U.S. government itself. I learned the right phrases, questions, and vocabulary.

Many times, if the target doesn't perceive the UCA as useful to his purposes from the beginning, the relationship will never make it to the next step. In these scenarios, perception is integral to the entire operation.

Balding Eagle was in his late fifties, so I found it useful to use my relative youth to advantage. He thought, or I led him to think, that I looked upon him as an experienced and wise elder statesman in the diplomatic community, and predictably he fed me questions that all too clearly revealed his intelligence agenda. Once I got past my pride, I realized he thought he'd hit a goldmine—a young and gullible bureaucrat who would "leak" all sorts of valuable inside information. Political intelligence doesn't have to be classified SECRET to be important to a hostile intelligence service; it need only be perceived as an accurate portrayal of the thinking of political insiders responsible for shaping foreign policy.

I realized that the best way for me to get the Balding Eagle to trust me was—act dumb. My pride balked at the ruse, and I resisted the act with every ounce of my being, but a job is a job and pretending dumbness was clearly the way to reach him. He thought he was smarter than I and treated me as though I was too stupid to see the true meaning behind his questions. He was condescending, too. I not only resented his attitude, my own attitude toward myself started to sag.

Intelligence is one of my personal values. This case, and this "dumb" approach, moved in a direction that ate away at my core beliefs about myself. I could not be authentic in my conversations with the Balding Eagle and felt like a second rate actor reading a very bad script.

> When I talked to my case agent, he listened intently to my concerns. And when I told him how I resented the Balding Eagle's arrogance, the case agent ended the conversation with two words: "Buck up."

This verbal slap in the face is exactly what I needed. I was willing to let a good case go down the drain because of my own pride! My attitude needed to change. I can't say it was easy, because the Balding Eagle was a chauvinistic opportunist who never treated me as an equal; he portrayed himself as someone with a superior intelligence and mission.

For each undercover identity, I used a name that was similar to my own. I insisted upon this after an incident where I was dining with the Balding Eagle at a local restaurant and a friend ran over to our table, calling me by my real name and asking about *work*. It has never ceased to amaze me why the Balding

Eagle didn't query me about my friend calling me by another name and her not-so-subtle references to *work*. To my astonishment, the Balding Eagle simply neglected to pay attention to bits of information that should have triggered suspicion about me in his mind.

Those kinds of mistakes were the result of inexperience and naiveté on my part as a young undercover agent (I stopped meeting targets at local restaurants), but the reaction from the Balding Eagle gave me insight into how we all form attitudes and develop opinions. He was a spy trained to notice details, and he should have paid attention, but I discovered that it was easier and more convenient for him to see me as malleable and inexperienced, so he let important clues about my real identity slip by unnoticed.

Every time we met, I turned into the young and gullible bureaucrat who inadvertently blurted out "disinformation" that he could scurry back with to the home office. Disinformation is a brilliant way of providing a foreign agent with information that actually sends them off track, at least for a while until they catch on. I knew my days were numbered with the Balding Eagle. Eventually, either or his superiors would become suspicious of my information and me.

In the meanwhile, as I harnessed the power of a positive attitude, I was learning what the Russians didn't know by the questions the Balding Eagle presented to me. This intelligence was forwarded to FBI Headquarters, which reported itself happy with the product we were producing.

I never knew what ultimately happened to the Balding Eagle. I do remember waving good-bye to him as he flew back to Moscow, thanking God and Aeroflot that he was gone from my life forever.

HOW TO CHANGE YOUR FUTURE

You can be more successful if you change your attitude.

My attitude became a self-limiting belief because I didn't think I could move beyond it. And it wouldn't have happened unless my case agent told me to "get over myself." It may have sounded harsh at first, but it was exactly what I needed to hear.

As human beings, we live in a continuous cycle, where our beliefs and results are inexorably linked. My beliefs were affecting my attitude. Since my attitude was not good, my performance was not as vigorous as it could have been.

You would be surprised at how many people hang on to beliefs that create failure instead of success. Self-limiting beliefs place you in a descending spiral—where failure becomes ever easier and acceptable. Positive beliefs, however, can place you in ascending spiral, where success becomes easier.

I was able to maintain a positive attitude. I continued to meet with the Balding Eagle, and because he was convinced of my inexperience and gullibility, his questions became increasingly transparent. We compromised every intelligence operation he initiated while in the United States.

U.S. AMY MILITARY RESILIENCE TRAINING PROGRAM

A positive attitude is the key to resilience.

Thirty years of research suggests that resilience can be measured and taught—and the U.S. Army is putting that idea to test in a program called Comprehensive Soldier Fitness (CSF). The goal of CSF is to make soldiers as fit psychologically as they are physically. The key component of this program involves resilience training that builds strong minds, strong strengths, and strong relationships.

Psychologist Martin Seligman, who is known for his theory of learned helplessness, developed the CSF program. Seligman met with army officials who were worried about the effects of Post Trauma Stress Disorder (PTSD). He explained that most people react with symptoms of depression and anxiety, but within a month or so are physically and psychologically back to where they were before the trauma. That is resilience.

There were a few individuals, however, who showed post-traumatic growth. They, too, first experience depression and anxiety, but within a year they are actually better off than they were before the trauma.

Seligman explained how the army could teach the psychological skills to shift the likelihood that soldiers would not just recover, but grow mental toughness, after a trauma.

It's not only the U.S. Army that has relied upon the "suck it up and move on" mentality that gets soldiers to overcome adversity. Many of us have grown up the same way, and we learned these coping techniques as children. Not everyone gets to play with the red ball on the playground. The ways in which we all learned to cope with crises like this as a child are the patterns we've leaned into as adults.

How we come out of adversity determines the way in which we can make ourselves a better person. Conflicts cannot always be won or lost by whoever has the biggest, fastest plane—or car, or whatever. Conflicts are won by having the smartest people with the strongest mind making the hard decisions in volatile environments.

Soldiers endure a rigorous physical fitness program in order to cope with the harsh environments of Iraq and Afghanistan. Seligman's CSF program teaches soldiers how to be in control of the thoughts and actions during events that are extremely difficult to handle. The program teaches how to counter the bias toward negativity in difficult and challenging situations: instead of giving in to a negative reaction, create positive emotions and attitudes. Soldiers are taught to search for positive experiences by thinking about why things went well and ways to create circumstances that enables good things to occur.

BE POSITIVE

These are the lessons about maintaining a positive attitude that I learned:

Search for positive experiences in difficult situations. No matter how dire the situation, I could always find something positive in it if I looked hard enough.

Identify what circumstances provided the positive experience. It was important to understand the circumstances in which I performed at my best so I could recognize them for what they were in the future.

Think about why things went well. I sought to understand why I performed with excellence in a hostile or pressurized environment. Was it the people around me who believed in me? Was it because I was alone with my own thoughts? What personal strength served me well in that situation? I worked hard to understand my environment—what was it about that environment that brought out the strength in me? Adversity presented challenges that beckoned me to push myself further.

Name the strengths that surfaced in the difficult situation. As I reviewed the situation, I thought about the strengths that moved me toward my goal. I focused only on the specific strengths that surfaced in the time of stress. I now owned those strengths and could call them back to action when faced with a similar situation in the future.

Pinpoint ways circumstances can be created next time to produce even better results. Now that I knew which circumstances brought out my best performance, I could begin to strategize on how to create similar circumstances for the future.

Create more learning situations where the positive traits and attitudes can be reinforced. After most joint operations with other federal agencies, the FBI brings everyone together to discuss what aspects of the operation went well. This is called a Hotwash and the purpose is to give constructive feedback to participants while memories are still fresh and vivid. To save face, it's tempting to posture and point the finger at others for mistakes and miscalculations, but this is not the intention of a Hotwash. The purpose is to identify individual and collective responses in the challenging situation so strengths can be reinforced and built upon for the next operation.

I attended one Hotwash while assigned as the spokesperson for the FBI in Northern California. The FBI had joined two other federal law enforcement agencies on a series of early morning arrests. In the Hotwash debriefing, I was asked to identify what went right in notifying the media and handling the public relations aspect. I was able to focus on how my positive attitude toward the media helped bridge the friction that sometimes exists between the press's right to information and law enforcement's desire to execute arrest and search warrants with a minimum of interference.

THINK LIKE AN OPTIMIST

This coincides with what behavioral scientists have been saying for years: mental toughness comes from thinking like an optimist.

People who don't give up have a habit of interpreting setbacks as temporary and changeable. When they encounter adversity, they believe that it is limited to one situation and that they can do something to change it.

If you have a strong mind, you have the skill to analyze your beliefs and emotions about failure. You can avoid describing failure as permanent, pervasive, and out of your control. This skill will build an internal strength that will enable you to focus and react to situations with more clarity and positive results.

It does not take talent or higher intelligence to be resilient. It can be taught, and it begins with a simple change of attitude—looking for the positive patterns and experiences and learning how to duplicate the attitudes and emotions that move you toward your goal.

You can think your way into failure and unhappiness, just as you can think your way into success and happiness. Your world is not controlled so much by outside circumstances as by your inner attitude. To change your circumstances, try thinking about them differently.

THINKING ABOUT POSITIVE ATTITUDE

Point to Ponder: A positive attitude is a choice you make every day.

Inspiration: *"Expect the best and get it."*—Norman Vincent Peale

Reflection Question: How has a positive attitude helped you bounce back after failure?

RESILIENCE TACTICS

ADVERSITY

Here are some things to keep in mind when facing adversity:

Press on. There is no other way to move forward. If your goals are really important to you, then do not give yourself any other choice other than to press on.

Remember the competition. If we are motivated to succeed, we look for ways to beat the competition. By knowing what the competition is doing, we can generate enthusiasm and excitement. Our success can be driven or influenced by the failure of our competitors. We can harness competitive knowledge while maintaining the focus on our own goals and objectives.

Love what you do. Overcoming adversity is much easier if we're doing something that matters to us. If the goal is important, the obstacles are not enough to turn us away.

Accept what you cannot change. Spend time on changing the things you can change and not trying to change those you can't.

Learn from the challenge. Failure is not the opposite of success—it is a part of success. Failure becomes success when you learn from it. If you change the way you look at things, the thing you look at changes. Instead of looking at what is missing and how far you still have to go, focus on what is present and how far you have come.

FAILURE

We all need to regain lost ground at times. Here are some things that have worked for me.

Focus on the problem, not the people. When something goes wrong, it's tempting to blame someone. A healthier approach is to focus on the processes that broke down rather than who failed. Stay with the problem and learn from it rather than put it behind you too quickly.

Allow yourself to fail on purpose. Set out to do something that you know has a good chance of failing, provided it won't harm others or have negative consequences. Learn something in which you have no talent or is beyond your area of expertise. You will gain several insights, including:

1. Learn how to handle failure with grace.

2. Recognize your limits.

3. Uncover real reasons for failure.

4. Extract key behavioral issues that may pop up again.

Forget how other people view you. Don't worry about what others think. It's easy to be an expert critic without having all the inside information. You will always be your own worst critic so don't waste time thinking about whether people are judging you. People who cling to negative and judgmental opinions are the ones you need to avoid.

POSITIVE ATTITUDE

Some people are born with the power of a positive attitude. Even if you were not born with one, it is a decision you can make every day. You choose whether to wake up grumpy or with a positive outlook on your life. Here are some skills to help you develop a positive attitude:

Look for opportunity in every difficulty. Take advantages of the opportunities as they present themselves. Why keep learning the same lesson over and over again? Get it right the first time so you can move on! Some people have 25 years of experience, while others have one year repeated 25 times. You decide which it will be.

Surround yourself with positive people. You are only as good as the company you keep. If you hang around gloomy and pessimistic people, guess what? Not only will you be sounding and looking like them—positive people won't want to have anything to do with you.

The key to success can be found through positive people who appreciate life and being happy. These people like to live in the moment and get joy from helping others. If you begin to surround yourself with people like this, you will see that you begin to improve the quality of your own life. Since the people that you choose to be around have a tremendous impact on your moods, it is all right to be picky when choosing friends. Even if you tend to be a negative person, being around people who are positive will help to alter the way in which you live your life.

Deliberately speak with hope. For the next twenty-four hours, deliberately speak and write with hope about your future. Go out of your way to convey your sense of hope and optimism about your job, family, and relationships. This may be difficult for you at first, but it will do two things: First, it will create a positive attitude; second, it will force you to find something positive in your life situation. Do not let words like realistic or inevitable sneak into your vocabulary when you're focusing on your future. When you say, "I'm just being realistic—I'll never get promoted" you are not being realistic; you are being negative. Instead, talk about ways you could change your circumstances so you can get noticed and promoted.

Feed your mind. Marcus Aurelius said, *"A man's life is what his thoughts make of it."* Shift your thinking from the negative to the positive. Just as you feed your body with nourishing food so you can perform at your best, feed your mind with healthy and wholesome thoughts.

Visualize success. Paint a mental picture of what success would look like for you. Visualize achievement. Hold firmly to a picture of success, not failure. An inflow of positive mental images of yourself in a place of achievement has the power to remake you as you approach every difficulty.

Meditate or pray daily. Start every day by expressing your gratitude for your life and your blessings in life. The secret to a more productive and successful life is to cast out negative thoughts and substitute them with new and dynamic ones.

CONCLUSION

Secrets of A Strong Mind has shown you how to uncover the personal strengths you will need to develop the strong character that leads to mental toughness. Whether overcoming a career or personal setback, recovering from loss or grief, setting a new challenge for yourself, or finding yourself in transition, the skills shared in this book will help you adapt, grow, and thrive.

My experiences as an FBI undercover and counterintelligence agent has shown me that many of my personal strengths were dormant until I found myself in situations where my fear was exposed. In many instances, the skills I needed to overcome these fears were developed in childhood. Others were developed as an adult.

I have shared many of my own stories with you, and while my background will be different from yours, your unique story has as much impact on your personality and behavior as mine has had on me. I encourage you to look at your own life a little closer to see what it has to teach you. Your experiences are powerful, and they have the ability to show you how to create the mental toughness you will need to move forward when plans fail and you find yourself in unexpected situations.

Your childhood experiences influence the way in which you look at your life now. It is important to recognize how these impressions affect your ability to be authentic, purposeful, courageous, confident, determined, and resilient.

As an adult, you have learned that you can't get better at overcoming disappointment just by working more hours for it. You don't lag behind in determination simply because you didn't start working on your determination project early enough. These are character traits that are not as easy to identify as IQ. They are developed through struggle and overcoming adversity.

The reason I included Tactics at the end of each chapter was to help you look deeper into your own life. Tactics are tools to help you pinpoint the instances when you developed the crucial ability to overcome real setbacks in life, and in the process, develop a strong mind. Excavate the lessons these incidents have to teach you.

The first person you need to lead is yourself. For this reason, leadership is a transformational journey. No matter where you are in life, the secrets to a strong mind can be found within you if you take the time to discover them. The character traits are there, ready to be excavated and polished. When you do, you will uncover the skills you need to lead a family, community group, church, small company, or a corporation.

When I was a teenager and began working in a local County Assessor's office, I came across this speech given at the Sorbonne in Paris by President Theodore Roosevelt. It made a lasting impression on me, and in closing, I would like to share it to encourage you.

246

"It is not the critic who counts; not the man who points out how the strong man stumbles, or where the doer of deeds could have done them better. The credit belongs to the man who is actually in the arena, whose face is marred by dust and sweat and blood; who strives valiantly; who errs, who comes short again and again, because there is no effort without error and shortcoming; but who does actually strive to do the deeds; who knows great enthusiasms, the great devotions; who spends himself in a worthy cause; who at the best knows in the end the triumph of high achievement, and who at the worst, if he fails, at least fails while daring greatly, so that his place shall never be with those cold and timid souls who neither know victory nor defeat."

—THEODORE ROOSEVELT

SOURCE NOTES

[1] Martin Seligman and Martin Matthews. *Comprehensive Soldier Fitness.* American Psychological Association, Vol. 66, (1), January, 2011.

[2] Don Richard Riso and Russ Hudson. *The Wisdom of the Enneagram: The Complete Guide to Psychological and Spiritual Growth for the Nine Personality Types.* Bantam Books, 1999.

[3] Matt Davis. *MRC Cognition and Brain Sciences.* Cambridge University, October 30, 2003.

[4] Genesis, Chapters 37, 39-47. *The Bible.*

[5] Daniel Wong. "Reflections of a Compulsive Goal Setter." *The Chronicle,* Duke University, April 6, 2011.

[6] Melinda Beck. "Anxiety Can Bring Out The Best." *Wall Street Journal,* June 18, 2012.

[7] Gregory Berns. "The Stupidity of Crowds." *Psychology Today,* September 23, 2008.

[8] Martin Seligman. *Authentic Happiness: Using Positive Psychology to Realize Your Potential for Lasting Fulfillment.* Free Press, 2003.

[9] Geoff Colvin. "Talent is Overrated: What Really Separates World Class Performers from Everyone Else." *Portfolio Trade,* 2010.

[10] First Book of Samuel, Chapter 17. *The Bible.*

[11] Seligman and Matthews. *Ibid.*

[12] Lolly Daskal. www.LollyDaskal.com.

[13] Benedict Carey. *"On the Road to Recovery, Past Adversity Provides A Map." New York Times, January 3, 2011.*